Apron Strings
Family
Cookbook

by Evy and Chick

Paws Press 1998
Atlantic Beach, Florida

·Printed in the United States of America

10 9 8 7 6 5 4 3 2 1

ISBN-0-9665219-0-0

Library of Congress Catalog Card Number: 98-66828

Paws Press
P.O. Box 331368
Atlantic Beach, Florida 32233

This Book is Dedicated to

Israel Van Buren Cox
Evelyn Marie Taylor Rupertis

Thank You

to **Beaches Arts Center**, Jacksonville Beach, Florida
*for offering to display and sell Apron Strings in their
gallery of beautiful paintings, pottery and glass works.*

*to friends, family and neighbors who brought recipes,
and childhood memories.*

to Nannette Martin for giving us her darling Elf drawing.

to Adele Gross for listening and listening.

*to Todd Gicalone for sharing his very favorite boyhood
recipe.*

to Fuzzy Walker for eating leftovers from recipe tests.

to Susanne Schuenke for encouragement.

*to the late Charlotte Reid, who brought "how to books"
and said "do it."*

Evy and Chick

CONTENTS

CREDITS

BILL BIERMAN	GRAPHIC DESIGN
ARLENE COX	ILLUSTRATIONS
RICHARD COX	COMPUTER WORK
VIRGINIA HUFFMAN	PROOFING
NANNETTE MARTIN	CELEBRATIONS "ELF"
ELIZABETH REED	EDITING

PRINTING BY:
PRINTCRAFT
JACKSONVILLE, FLORIDA

ILLUSTRATIONS

INTRODUCTION

If someone had told us as we lovingly gazed at our first born little darling that from bottle to 16 years, we would be responsible for feeding him over 17,000 meals, we would have turned into raving maniacs. Anyway, babies cast magic spells on parents. All we wanted to know then was how we could fulfill his every need immediately. The earth should have opened up and swallowed us, but it didn't. We continued to have more darlings until we witnessed our first teen feeding frenzy and that part of our life was over. We had come a long way. We learned a lot--fast. One thing we learned was that between Grandma's dining table overloaded with bowl after bowl of food and throwing a bag of fast food on the table, lies a middle ground when feeding the family.

In turn, they have learned how to sit at the table, how to eat their food in a socially acceptable way, how to use the proper utensils. They learned very young that we were not short order cooks. There was no way we could preserve our dignity and take orders from a scruffy little darling with dirty fingernails and an undeveloped palate tickled only by catsup and mustard. They also learned that the dinner table was not an extension of the playground, meals were not races, none of us was deaf, and dessert was last.

One little darling liked everything. He became a politician. One liked almost nothing, our rebel.

The ones in between were "good" eaters. Over the years they all flourished and we survived. Now we are home cooking for a new generation.

Before memory fails, we are happy to share with you some of the "middle ground" that worked for us. Have fun feeding your family; we did. And get a dog. No vacuum cleaner can outdo a dog in keeping the dining room carpet clean.

Evy and Chick

MAIN DISHES

BEEF and CABBAGE CASSEROLE

1	LB. HAMBURGER
1	SM. ONION, CHOPPED
1	SM. CABBAGE, SLICED
2	C. SHARP CHEDDAR, SHREDDED
1	C. BEEF STOCK
1	14½ OZ. CAN TOMATOES, CHOPPED
1	8 OZ. CAN TOMATO SAUCE
1	C. INSTANT RICE
1	C. GREEN PEPPER, CHOPPED, OPTIONAL

BROWN AND CRUMBLE MEAT. PUT INSTANT RICE
IN BOTTOM OF OILED CASSEROLE. LAYER MEAT,
CABBAGE, TOMATOES, CHEDDAR, AND PEPPER.
ADD BEEF STOCK. TOP WITH TOMATO SAUCE.
COVER. BAKE AT 350° ABOUT AN HOUR UNTIL
BUBBLY.

*Reminiscent of traditional cabbage rolls. Easy
for darlings to do, even with telephones stuck
to their ears.*

BEEF STROGANOFF

1	LB. SIRLOIN STEAK
2	TBS. OLIVE OIL
1	TBS. BUTTER
1½	C. ONION, CHOPPED
¼	TSP. DILL WEED
1	TBS. FLOUR
2	TSP. DRY MUSTARD
2	C. MUSHROOMS, SLICED
2	C. BEEF STOCK
½	PINT SOUR CREAM OR SOUR HALF AND HALF
1	PKG. NOODLES

HEAT OIL AND BUTTER IN A LARGE SKILLET.
BROWN MEAT AND ONION. ADD STOCK AND
MUSHROOMS. COVER. SIMMER ABOUT 1 HR.
THICKEN GRAVY WITH FLOUR.

COOK NOODLES ACCORDING TO PACKAGE
DIRECTIONS. PLACE NOODLES AROUND THE
EDGE OF A LARGE, WARMED SERVING DISH.
PUT BEEF IN CENTER. MIX SOUR CREAM,
MUSTARD, AND DILL WEED. PLACE SOUR CREAM
ON CENTER OF BEEF PLATTER OR SERVE
SEPARATELY.

*We never found a reason for the "little
darling" to see a whole steak until they were
about to leave the nest. College graduation
seemed like a good time to treat them to a steak
dinner while untying the apron strings.*

3

SPAGHETTI and MEAT BALLS

3   **POUNDS GROUND BEEF CHUCK**
2   **EGGS, BEATEN,**
    CRACKER MEAL
    SALT AND PEPPER TO TASTE

MIX EGGS INTO MEAT.
ADD ENOUGH MEAL TO MAKE A STIFF MIXTURE.
FORM INTO BALLS, ROLLING AND PATTING TO
REMOVE AIR POCKETS . MAKES ABOUT 12
DEPENDING ON THE SIZE YOU DESIRE. SET ASIDE
IN REFRIGERATOR.

SPAGHETTI SAUCE

1   **PINT OLIVE OIL**
1   **6 POUND CAN TOMATOES**
2   **18 OZ. CANS TOMATO PASTE**
8   **CUPS ONIONS CHOPPED**
⅛   **CUP GARLIC CHOPPED OR TO TASTE**
4   **BAY LEAVES**

HEAT OIL IN A LARGE ROASTER PAN, BROWN
MEAT BALLS. REMOVE FROM PAN. ADD ONIONS
AND GARLIC TO PAN. COOK UNTIL SOFT. ADD
TOMATOES, TOMATO PASTE AND BAY LEAVES.
STIR WELL. RETURN BROWNED MEAT BALLS,
PUSHING THEM DOWN INTO SAUCE. COVER PAN.
COOK OVERNIGHT IN A SLOW OVEN, 250° OR 300°,
UNTIL TOMATOES AND ONIONS ARE COOKED
INTO A DARK, RICH SAUCE. SKIM EXCESS OIL FROM
SAUCE.

*Freezes extremely well. Grandpa likes the sauce
on scrambled eggs. Most "little darlings" love
spaghetti, and all need spaghetti bibs.*

BRISKET 1

1   **4 TO 5 LB. BRISKET**
1   **LARGE ONION, SLICED**
1   **C. CHILI SAUCE**
1   **CAN OF BEER**
1   **C. BEEF BROTH**
1   **TBS. HORSERADISH**

COMBINE CHILI SAUCE, BEER, BROTH, AND HORSE-
RADISH. POUR OVER BRISKET. TOP MEAT WITH
ONION SLICES. COVER. BAKE 350° UNTIL TENDER,
ABOUT 30 MIN. TO THE POUND.

BRISKET 2

COOK BRISKET WITH A SMALL AMOUNT OF BROTH
AND SOME ONION. WHEN DONE, COOL, SLICE
ACROSS GRAIN AND RETURN TO PAN.
REFRIGERATE OVER NIGHT. POUR BAR B.Q. SAUCE
OVER MEAT. BAKE 1 HOUR AT 350° BASTING OFTEN
WITH SAUCE.

*When "teen darling" displayed symptoms of never
being filled up, no cruise company was willing to
take them for an extended cruise. We learned to
roast large pieces of meat. Hopefully a few scraps
would be left over for sandwiches. Sandwiches are
snack food to
teenagers.*

5

MEAT LOAF

1	LB. GROUND BEEF
½	LB. SAUSAGE MEAT
1	LARGE ONION, CHOPPED
2	CLOVES GARLIC, CHOPPED
2	STALKS CELERY, CHOPPED
1	EGG
1½	C. BREAD CRUMBS
¼	C. MILK
½	C. CHILI SAUCE
1	TSP. SALT
¼	TSP. PEPPER
1	8 OZ. CAN TOMATO SAUCE

MIX IN A LARGE BOWL. PRESS INTO GREASED LOAF PAN. BAKE 1 HOUR AT 350°. POUR TOMATO SAUCE OVER TOP AND COOK 30 MINUTES LONGER.

The first "big darling" in the door from school can get this in the oven.

STUFFWICHES

Enter a "little darling" and a troop of friends with that look of hunger in their eyes. Our status demands keeping panic concealed. A well-stocked pantry helps. Send them on their way to the picnic table or porch with a tray of stuffwiches and a bag of chips.

8   **HAMBURGER BUNS**
1   **12 OUNCE CAN CORNED BEEF, SHREDDED**
8   **SLICES OF CHEESE**
½   **CUP BARBEQUE SAUCE**
8   **SLICES OF ONION AND GREEN PEPPER RINGS**

SHRED CORNED BEEF AND HEAT WITH SAUCE. DIVIDE MEAT BETWEEN ROLLS; ADD CHEESE AND WRAP EACH IN FOIL. HEAT IN 350° OVEN FOR 15 MINUTES.

DEVILED STUFFED HAMBURGER

1   **POUND GROUND BEEF**
1   **EGG**
1   **TSP. WORCESTERSHIRE SAUCE**
1   **TSP. MINCED ONION**
2   **TSP. HORSERADISH**
1   **TSP. PREPARED MUSTARD**
½   **C. BREAD CRUMBS**
¼   **C. DRY RED WINE**
1   **TSP. TABASCO SAUCE**
6   **½ INCH CUBES OF CHEESE**

COMBINE ALL EXCEPT CHEESE. DIVIDE INTO SIX PORTIONS. FORM EACH PORTION AROUND A PIECE OF CHEESE.

Grill, broil or fry.

7

1   **LB. HAMBURGER**
1   **CUP CORN RELISH**
6   **HOT DOG ROLLS**
6   **SLICES SWISS CHEESE**

BROWN HAMBURGER AND CRUMBLE. MIX WITH
RELISH. PLACE OPENED ROLLS ON A COOKIE SHEET.
SCOOP EXCESS DOUGH OUT OF ONE SIDE; LIGHTLY
TOAST. REMOVE FROM BROILER. STUFF SCOOPED
OUT SIDE WITH MEAT MIXTURE. TOP BOTH SIDES
WITH CHEESE. RETURN TO BROILER TO MELT
CHEESE. FOLD SIDES TOGETHER.

*It's not fancy, but it is beloved by "teenage
darlings." Of course they can do it themselves.
We've even seen them get quite creative with
this recipe by adding onions, olives, mashed
potatoes or any left overs not tied down in the
fridge. We love it when they express their
creativity in quiet ways.*

CHUCK WAGON SCRAMBLED EGGS

12 **EGGS**
½ **LB. BACON, FRIED, CRUMBLED**
1½ **C. SALSA**
1 **CAN SPICY PINTO BEANS, HEATED**
2 **C. GRATED LONGHORN CHEESE**
1 **C. SOUR CREAM**
2 **TBS. CHIVES**

HEAT A LARGE PLATTER IN A 200° OVEN. BEAT
EGGS UNTIL LIGHT AND FLUFFY. SCRAMBLE IN A
SMALL AMOUNT OF OIL OR FAT FROM BACON. TO
ASSEMBLE FOR SERVING, PLACE COOKED EGGS IN
THE CENTER OF THE PLATTER. SPREAD BEANS
AND BACON AROUND EGGS. PUT SALSA DOWN
THE CENTER AND SPRINKLE ALL WITH CHEESE.
RETURN TO OVEN TO MELT CHEESE. MIX CHIVES
AND SOUR CREAM. SERVE SEPARATELY.

SMASHED POTATO DOGS

1 **PKG. HOT DOGS, BOILED**
1½ **C. MASHED POTATOES**
10 **SLICES AMERICAN CHEESE**

SPLIT HOT DOGS; COVER WITH POTATOES. FOLD
CHEESE SLICE IN HALF, PLACE ON POTATOES.
BAKE UNTIL CHEESE IS MELTED.

*Great chefs might weep but this is the meal of choice
for one "little darling". Wonderful melange of
easy, economical and quick. Try it, you'll like it!*

GLORIOUS GOOP
A geographical treat

The perfect answer to that question, genetically imprinted on a brain cell before birth, "What's for dinner?"--is, without hesitation--GOOP, wash your hands and set the table please. Goop is family fare par excellence. Goop is fast, easy, cheap, flexible, good and filling. It can be your favorite ethnic food flavor. With an open mind and spice cabinet, the possibilities are endless.

BASIC INGREDIENTS
1 **LB. HAMBURGER, BROWNED. ADD**
2 **FRESH OR 1 CAN DICED TOMATOES. ADD**
½ **C. BEEF BROTH AND INGREDIENTS OF CHOICE .**
1 **12 OZ. PKG. PASTA OR NOODLES.** COOK SEPARATELY AND TOSS WITH HAMBURGER BEFORE SERVING.

POSSIBILITIES

ITALIAN

FENNEL SEEDS, ONION, BASIL
GREEN PEPPER, OREGANO
TOP WITH CHEESE.

GREEK

MUSHROOMS, OLIVES,
GARLIC, FETA CHEESE.

GERMAN
CABBAGE, CELERY,
CARAWAY SEEDS.

ALL AMERICAN
CORN, ZUCCHINI
TARRAGON, PEAS
BEANS, ONIONS.

GARDEN POTPOURRI CASSEROLE

1½ C. INSTANT RICE, UNCOOKED
1½ C. CORN, CUT FROM COB
1 C. ZUCCHINI, SLICED
1 LG. ONION, SLICED
1 MED. GREEN PEPPER, CHOPPED
4 MED. TOMATOES, SLICED
1 LB. SMOKED, FULLY COOKED SAUSAGE,
  DIAGONALLY SLICED
1½ C. VEGETABLE BROTH
1 TSP. CILANTRO
1 TSP. CELERY SEEDS
1 TSP. BUTTER
1½ C. MONTEREY JACK CHEESE, GRATED

LAYER IN AN OILED CASSEROLE IN THE FOLLOWING ORDER
    RICE, SPRINKLE WITH CILANTRO AND
    CELERY SEED
    CORN, DOT WITH BUTTER
    ONION
    2 TOMATOES, TOP WITH GREEN PEPPER
½ MEAT
    ZUCCHINI
2 TOMATOES
    REMAINING MEAT
    POUR VEGETABLE BROTH OVER CASSEROLE

Cover, bake 350° 45 minutes.
Uncover, add cheese; bake 15 minutes.

11

BAKED HAM STEAK

4 HAM STEAKS
½ C. ORANGE MARMALADE
¼ C. MAPLE SYRUP
GROUND CLOVES TO TASTE

CLIP EDGES OF STEAKS TO KEEP THEM FLAT.
PLACE IN OVEN PAN. SPRINKLE WITH CLOVES.
COAT EACH STEAK WITH WARMED MARMALADE.
DRIBBLE MAPLE SYRUP OVER MARMALADE.
COVER PAN. BAKE 350° FOR 1 HOUR, DEPENDING
ON THICKNESS OF MEAT. BASTE. COOK 15 MIN.
UNCOVERED TO THICKEN GLAZE.

Serve with french fried sweet potatoes and chunky apple sauce. "Little darlings" like a little vanilla flavoring in their applesauce.

CHICKS LAZY CHUCK

1 3 LB. CHUCK ROAST
1 PKG. ONION-MUSHROOM SOUP MIX
1 SMALL CAN TOMATO SAUCE
1 SMALL CAN WATER OR RED WINE

MAY USE: POTATOES   CARROTS
**   TURNIPS   ONIONS**

BAKE ROAST WITH SOUP MIX, SAUCE AND WINE,
COVERED, 1½ HR. AT 350°. ADD VEGETABLES OF
CHOICE. RE-COVER; BAKE 30 MIN. OR UNTIL
VEGETABLES ARE TENDER. REMOVE TO PLATTER.
THICKEN PAN JUICES FOR GRAVY.

LITTLE DARLING BISCUITS

Chick says, "Busy is happy." Making, baking, and then eating still warm biscuits oozing with jelly is a happy way for a team of darlings to keep busy on a rainy day.

Provide basic biscuit dough, rolling pins, cutters, beaten egg yolks and a variety of seeds for decoration. Try celery, sesame, caraway, poppy and anise seeds.

Give instructions: "Roll, cut, brush with egg yolk, (the glue of the cooking world), sprinkle with seeds. Place in pan. All that re-rolling and re-shaping does make the dough a little tough and a little grey but no one cares. The creations will be theirs and will be beautiful.

We do not suggest you leave the kitchen, but try staying calm and out of the way. They make, you may help bake. Conserve strength to help with clean up.

They ate biscuits with sausage patties for the main course followed by biscuits with jelly for dessert. Nothing tough about menu planning for "darlings."

"THE BEST BISCUIT THEY EVER ATE."

Grandpa likes biscuits with everything. Kids do too.

INTO CROCK POT PUT

CHICK'S CHIVE CHICKEN

- **2 TBS. BUTTER**
- **2 CLOVES GARLIC**
- **½ CUP WHITE WINE OR VERMOUTH**
- **½ CUP CHICKEN BROTH**
- **1 CHICKEN, CUT UP**
   SALT AND PEPPER

WHEN DONE REMOVE CHICKEN, REDUCE BROTH TO
¼ CUP, ADD ¾ CUP SOUR CREAM, 2 TBS. CHIVES
POUR SAUCE OVER CHICKEN AND SERVE WITH RICE
OR NOODLES.

*A good time to use the crock pot is when you
want to see a little darling play ball all afternoon.
Another good time is when the cook is busy reading a
juicy novel. Chick gets lots of compliments from the
little darlings on his culinary skills with this dish,
especially at allowance time. The wine won't hurt the
"little darlings." Heat destroys the alcohol.*

14

CROCK POT

PORK and SAUERKRAUT

3	**LBS. SAUERKRAUT, RINSED**
2	**LBS. CUBED PORK**
1	**MED. ONION**
½	**C. WHITE WINE**
1	**CAN BEEF BROTH**
1	**TSP. CARAWAY SEED**
1	**TBS. JUNIPER BERRIES**
2	**TBS. OIL**

BROWN MEAT AND ONION IN A SKILLET. PUT
SAUERKRAUT, WINE, BEEF BROTH, SEEDS AND
BERRIES IN CROCK POT. TOP WITH MEAT AND
ONIONS. SIMMER UNTIL MEAT IS TENDER AND
FLAVORS BLENDED.

Serve with brown mustard

*Put brown mustard in an English mustard pot
with tiny spoon. Little hands love little containers.
Much mustard will be used by diners.*

PORK CHOPS with CORNBREAD STUFFING

6   CHOPS, CENTER CUT
1   BOX CORNBREAD STUFFING MIX
1   TBS. DRIED ONION FLAKES

MAKE STUFFING A LITTLE MORE MOIST THAN
CALLED FOR IN THE DIRECTIONS ON THE BOX.
PLACE A MOUND OF COOLED DRESSING ON EACH
CHOP. LAY CHOPS IN   SHALLOW PAN. ADD ½ INCH
OF WATER WITH ONION FLAKES. COVER, BAKE 350°.
LAST 15 MIN. BAKE UNCOVERED TO CRISP TOP OF
DRESSING.

*We tried putting the stuffing into pockets in the
chops, but all darlings complained "not enough
dressing" except the one who just eats the meat. He
had a good barter item! One precious tiny darling
only wanted to eat the dressing until he was able to
eat several chops in his teen years. When raising
" darlings,"change is constant and irony is always.*

QUICK TOMATO SOUP

1   CAN CHICKEN BROTH
1   CAN WHOLE TOMATOES
1   TSP. BUTTER
DILL WEED, SALT AND PEPPER TO TASTE.

LIQUIFY TOMATOES IN BLENDER, ADD TO HOT
BROTH. SIMMER 15 MIN. SEASON AND SERVE.

16

CHICKEN LEGS CACCIATORE

5	LBS. CHICKEN LEGS
¼	C. OLIVE OIL
1	TBS. BUTTER
1	C. FLOUR
	SALT AND PEPPER
2	GREEN PEPPERS, SLICED
2	LARGE ONIONS. CHOPPED
4	CLOVES GARLIC, SLICED
2	14.5 OZ. CANS CHOPPED TOMATOES
¾	C. RED WINE
1	6 OZ. CAN TOMATO PASTE
1	TSP. OREGANO
½	TSP. THYME

PUT FLOUR, SALT, AND PEPPER IN A PAPER BAG.
SHAKE THE LEGS IN BAG UNTIL COATED. IN A LARGE
PAN, BROWN LEGS IN OIL AND HOT BUTTER.
REMOVE LEGS FROM PAN. ADD ONIONS, GARLIC,
AND PEPPERS. COOK UNTIL TENDER. ADD REMAINING
INGREDIENTS, LEGS AND ANY JUICES THAT
HAVE COLLECTED FROM THEM. BAKE 350° FOR 1 HR.
SERVE WITH GARLIC BREAD.

*"May I be excused please" is not heard as long as
the legs hold out.*

17

HOT CHILI and PEANUT CHICKEN

- 1 LARGE CHICKEN, CUT UP
- 2 TBS. SALT
- 2 TBS. GROUND GINGER
- ½ C. PEANUT OIL
- 1 C. ONION, CHOPPED
- 3 CLOVES GARLIC
- 1½ TSP. GRATED FRESH GINGER
- 1 CAN TOMATOES, CHOPPED
- 4 C. BOILING WATER, RESERVE ONE CUP
- 8 OZ. TOMATO SAUCE
- 2 WHOLE FRESH, HOT CHILIS, SEEDED
- 1 C. PEANUT BUTTER, BLENDED UNTIL SMOOTH WITH RESERVE WATER,
- ½ C. CHOPPED PEANUTS
- ½ C. CHOPPED BLACK OLIVES

RUB SALT & GROUND GINGER ONTO CHICKEN, BROWN IN THE HOT OIL. SET ASIDE IN A BOWL. DRAIN ALL BUT ¼ C. OIL FROM PAN AND ADD ONIONS, GARLIC AND FRESH GINGER. COOK UNTIL SOFT AND LIGHTLY BROWN. ADD TOMATOES AND TOMATO SAUCE. COOK 5 MINUTES, THEN SLOWLY STIR IN THE BOILING WATER. ADD CHILIS AND CHICKEN PIECES. COOK SLOWLY, UNCOVERED, 15 MINUTES. STIR IN PEANUT BUTTER PASTE AND CONTINUE TO COOK ABOUT 1 HR. PLACE IN HEATED DISH.

Garnish with
chopped peanuts and
black olives.

AWESOME !!!

18

PORK ROAST with LIMA BEANS

1   **PORK ROAST**
1   **LARGE ONION, CHOPPED**
1   **TSP. CELERY SEED**
1   **C. CATSUP**
5   **1 LB. CANS DRIED, COOKED LIMAS**
    SALT AND PEPPER TO TASTE

PUT ROAST IN A LARGE PAN WITH THE CHOPPED
ONION. ADD AN INCH OF WATER OR STOCK. COVER.
BAKE 350° UNTIL HALF DONE. TURN ROAST. ADD
BEANS, CATSUP, CELERY SEED AND CONTINUE
COOKING UNTIL ROAST IS WELL DONE AND GRAVY
HAS THICKENED.

A meal guaranteed to thaw frozen skaters,
including the one that got hit by the puck and
outdid most actresses with her performance.

EASY BLACK BEAN SOUP

1   **15 OZ. CAN BLACK BEANS**
1½   **C. BEEF BOUILLON**
½   **C. ONION AND CELERY**
1   **CLOVE GARLIC**
1   **TBS. LEMON JUICE**
      SALT AND PEPPER TO TASTE

BLEND ALL INGREDIENTS IN FOOD PROCESSOR.
SIMMER 15 MIN. ADD LEMON JUICE. SERVE.
GARNISH WITH THIN SLICE OF LEMON OR DOLLOP
OF SOUR CREAM.

BUTTERFLIED LEG OF LAMB
WITH KASHA

LEG OF LAMB, SHANK HALF. HAVE BUTCHER
REMOVE THE BONE, SPREADING ROAST FLAT.

BASTING SAUCE

⅓ **C. OLIVE OIL**
1 **TBS. SOY SAUCE**
¼ **C. RED WINE**
½ **TSP. ROSEMARY**
½ **TSP. GARLIC POWDER**
½ **TSP. BLACK PEPPER**

PREHEAT OVEN TO 425°. BRUSH BASTING SAUCE ON
BOTH SIDES OF ROAST. PLACE UNCOVERED ON A
RACK IN A SHALLOW PAN. COOK TO DESIRED
DONENESS, BASTING FREQUENTLY. REMOVE TO HOT
PLATTER. LET REST 10 MIN.

KASHA

1 **C. KASHA**   *Roasted Buckwheat Kernels*
1 **LB. SMALL MUSHROOMS**
3 **SMALL ONIONS, HALVED**
½ **C. SLICED ALMONDS**
2 **TBS. BUTTER**

FOLLOW BASIC RECIPE ON THE KASHA BOX. TO
ROASTING PAN JUICES ADD BUTTER, MUSHROOMS,
ONION AND ALMONDS. SAUTE. TOSS GENTLY WITH
COOKED KASHA.

*A ring of tiny cherry tomatoes around the kasha
makes a colorful garnish. Wonderful aromas bring
all the "darlings" to the table.*

20

LAMB SHANKS

6 LAMB SHANKS
1 C. VERMOUTH
1 C. BEEF STOCK
3 CLOVES GARLIC, SLICED
1 TBS. SOY SAUCE
PEPPER TO TASTE

BROWN SHANKS IN SMALL AMOUNT OF
OLIVE OIL IF DESIRED. ARRANGE IN A SINGLE LAYER
IN LARGE BAKING DISH.   ADD SEASONINGS. COVER,
BAKE 1 HR. AT 350°. TURN SHANKS. BASTE.
CONTINUE COOKING UNTIL MEAT IS TENDER.
PAN JUICES MAKE A RICH GRAVY FOR MASHED
POTATOES.

*"Can I eat this like we ate turkey legs at the
outdoor fair?" When the darlings first stood
upright, we learned to enunciate the word* **NO**
*clearly and they learned the definition. Always
trying to increase their vocabulary, we also
introduced the word* **appropriate.**

*Junior size eating utensils help deal with cutting
and hitting the mouth.*

21

HOT and SOUR SOUP

A miracle of blended flavors, a one pot meal.
Have all ingredients ready before starting to cook because cooking time is very short, 10 min. max.

8	**C. CHICKEN STOCK**
½	**LB. CHICKEN, CUT IN THIN STRIPS**
½	**LB. CURED HAM, SHREDDED**
4	**WOOD EARS, SOAKED IN BOILING WATER UNTIL SOFT, DRAINED AND SLICED**
1	**12 OZ. PKG. TOFU CUT IN STRIPS**
1	**8 OZ. CAN BAMBOO SHOOTS, SLICED**
1	**8 OZ. CAN WATER CHESTNUTS, SLICED**
2	**C. SNOW PEAS, CUT IN STRIPS**
2	**C. CHINESE CABBAGE, SHREDDED**

1	**TBS. SOY SAUCE,**	⅔	**C. CATSUP,**
1	**TBS. HOT SAUCE**	¾	**C. WHITE VINEGAR**
2	**TSP. SUGAR**	2	**TBS. CORNSTARCH**

Bring stock to boil. Add chicken and ham. Cook 5 min. Add vegetables and seasonings. Reduce heat to simmer. Cook another 5 min. Dissolve cornstarch in small amount of water. Add to soup, stirring until thickened.

TO FINISH

2   **EGGS, BEATEN**

Dribble eggs into soup while stirring fast.

6   **GREEN ONIONS FOR GARNISH**
    SESAME SEED OIL

Garnish each bowl with ½ tsp. sesame oil and sliced green onions. At the Oriental market the "little darlings" purchased china soup spoons, cups without handles, green tea in a lovely tin, a box of fortune cookies, and a can of lichee fruit. Shopping was fun and dinner was complete

22

GRANDMA'S PENN. DUTCH POTATO SOUP

3 **MED. POTATOES, DICED**
1 **MED. ONION, DICED**
3 **STALKS CELERY, CHOPPED**
5 **C. WATER**
   SALT AND PEPPER TO TASTE

BRING TO A BOIL AND COOK IN COVERED PAN
20 MIN. STIR RIVVELS INTO POT.

RIVVELS

¾ **C. FLOUR**
½ **TSP. SALT**
1 **BEATEN EGG**

MIX WITH FORK UNTIL CRUMBLY AND FAIRLY SMALL.
WHEN SOUP WITH RIVVELS HAS COOKED
20 MIN.

ADD:

1½ **C. MILK**
2   **TBS. BUTTER**

SIMMER 10 MIN.

This delicious soup sure fills up the "little darlings" on a cold night. To serve with this, they like that wonderful main dish, grilled ham sandwiches.
A dish of vegetable sticks rounds out the meal.

When a droopy drawers little darling is toddling around underfoot, something that can cook without much attention is a good idea.

LENTIL SOUP with HOT DOGS

1½ C. LENTILS
8 C. WATER OR STOCK
1 LARGE ONION, CHOPPED
2 HAM HOCKS
½ TSP. THYME
1 STALK CELERY, CHOPPED
1 BAY LEAF
1 FRESH TOMATO, CHOPPED
1 POTATO, CUBED
1 PKG. HOT DOGS

BRING ALL INGREDIENTS TO A BOIL EXCEPT HOT DOGS. REDUCE HEAT TO SIMMER. TURN ATTENTION TO LITTLE DARLING. CHECK SOUP IN ONE HOUR. CONTINUE ROUTINE UNTIL YOU OR THE LITTLE DARLING IS WORN OUT. WHEN SOUP IS DONE, REMOVE MEAT FROM HOCKS, RETURNING MEAT TO POT. TAKE NAP. AT DINNER TIME SLICE HOT DOGS; ADD TO SOUP. COOK UNTIL SLICES ARE DONE AND SOUP IS BUBBLING HOT.

CHILE CON CARNE

2   LB. GROUND VENISON, ELK, BUFFALO OR
     BEEF HEART
1   C. GREEN PEPPER, CHOPPED
2   C. ONION, CHOPPED
¼   C. OLIVE OIL
½   TSP. GARLIC SALT
2½ C. TOMATOES
2   CANS KIDNEY BEANS, MORE IF YOU DESIRE
     SALT AND PEPPER TO TASTE

BROWN MEAT IN OIL. ADD ONIONS AND PEPPERS.
CONTINUE TO COOK UNTIL VEGETABLES ARE
TENDER. ADD THE REST OF THE INGREDIENTS,
SIMMERING ABOUT 45 MINUTES.
SERVE WITH TORTILLA CHIPS.

Serve it. Don't explain it. It's delicious and low fat.

PEANUT SOUP

2½ C. CHICKEN OR VEGETABLE BROTH
3   TBS. BUTTER
3   TBS. FLOUR
1   SMALL ONION, MINCED
2   STALKS CELERY, SLICED THIN
½   C. CHUNKY PEANUT BUTTER
2   TSP. LEMON JUICE
¼   TSP. SALT

SAUTE CELERY AND ONION IN BUTTER. BLEND IN
FLOUR UNTIL ABSORBED. STIR IN BROTH, THEN
PEANUT BUTTER. ADD LEMON JUICE. SIMMER

*Garnish bowls with popcorn, except Grandma's.
She prefers her popcorn in front of the T.V.*

PORK and SHRIMP FRIED RICE

5	C. COLD COOKED RICE
6	COOKED SHRIMP, SLICED THIN
1	C. PORK, RAW, CUT IN THIN STRIPS
1	CARROT, CUT IN THIN STRIPS
1	GREEN PEPPER, CUT IN SMALL STRIPS
1	MED. ONION, CHOPPED
2	EGGS, BEATEN
¼	C. PEANUT OIL
1	TBS. SOY SAUCE

IN A LARGE PAN, HEAT OIL, STIR FRY PORK STRIPS, ADD CARROTS, ONION, GREEN PEPPER, FRYING UNTIL JUST CRISP. PUSH PORK AND VEGETABLES TO ONE SIDE OF PAN. ADD EGGS AND SCRAMBLE. MIX SCRAMBLED EGG AND VEGETABLES TOGETHER, ADD SHRIMP. FOLD IN RICE UNTIL ALL IS WELL MIXED. ADD SOY SAUCE. REMOVE TO LARGE WARMED PLATTER. CAN BE GARNISHED WITH SLICED GREEN ONION TOPS.

Little darlings think they are indulging in very exotic fare when they eat this dish.

SEAFOOD

PICKLED OYSTERS

1	PINT OYSTERS
¼	C. OLIVE OIL
10	DRIED RED PEPPERS
1	TBS. LIME JUICE
1	TBS. BALSAMIC VINEGAR
¼	TSP. SALT

DRAIN OYSTERS; SPREAD ON PAPER TOWELS TO
ABSORB EXCESS LIQUID. HEAT OIL. SLOWLY COOK
PEPPERS UNTIL CHARRED BLACK. DISCARD PEPPERS.
FRY OYSTERS IN THE SEASONED OIL. REMOVE
FROM HEAT ADD REMAINING INGREDIENTS.

Try as a first course. Garnish with capers.

HOT OYSTER POPPERS

1	PINT OYSTERS
¼	C. OLIVE OIL
4	CLOVES GARLIC
¼	C. HOT PEPPER SAUCE
1	TBS. BALSAMIC VINEGAR
	SALT AND PEPPER TO TASTE

DRAIN AND FRY OYSTERS IN OIL.
REMOVE FROM HEAT. ADD
REST OF INGREDIENTS. PUT
ALL IN GLASS CONTAINER AND
MARINATE SEVERAL DAYS.

*This is adult fare. Serve with
plain crackers and cold beer to
adult football viewers. Not
recommended for tiny tummies.*

SEAFOOD CASSEROLE
MIX and MATCH

1 **LB. SHRIMP, COOKED**
1 **LB. FRESH CRAB MEAT**
1 **MED. ONION, CHOPPED**
1 **C. CELERY, CHOPPED**
1¼ **C. MAYONNAISE**
1 **TBS. OIL**
1 **TSP. WORCESTERSHIRE SAUCE**
2 **TBS. BUTTER**
1 **8 OZ. PKG. HERB STUFFING MIX, DIVIDED**

SAUTE VEGETABLES IN OIL. RESERVE 1 CUP
STUFFING MIX. TO REMAINING STUFFING
ADD VEGETABLES AND SEAFOOD. STIR
WORCESTERSHIRE INTO MAYONNAISE. ADD TO
HERB-SEAFOOD MIX. PUT INTO OILED CASSEROLE.
MELT 2 TBS. BUTTER TOSS WITH THE RESERVED
CUP OF HERB MIX. TOP CASSEROLE WITH THE
BUTTERED CRUMBS.

BAKE 325° FOR 20 MIN. OR UNTIL HOT THROUGHOUT.

*You may substitute for the fresh crab meat, 2-6 oz.
cans of crabmeat off the grocery shelf or the
following:*

½ **POUND SCALLOPS AND**
½ **POUND FISH OR ANY COMBINATION
OF SEAFOOD YOU DESIRE**

*Mutiny may be declared by the whole family if
shrimp are not included in the casserole. We
tried it once. The love of shrimp runs deep.*

29

OYSTER PIE

1 **QUART OYSTERS**
½ **C. FLOUR, SEASONED WITH SALT AND PEPPER**
3 **SLICES BACON, DICED**
1 **TBS. PARSLEY, MINCED**
1 **TBS. GREEN PEPPER, MINCED**
1 **SMALL ONION, CHOPPED**
½ **TSP. PAPRIKA**
  PINCH OF CAYENNE
1 **LEMON, JUICED**
2 **TBS. CREAM**
2 **TSP. BUTTER**
1 **TUBE OF READY MADE BISCUITS**

DRAIN OYSTERS. ROLL EACH ONE IN FLOUR. PLACE HALF OF THE OYSTERS CLOSE TOGETHER IN A SINGLE LAYER IN A BUTTERED SHALLOW BAKING DISH. SAUTE ONION AND BACON. SPRINKLE ½ OF THE BACON, ONION, GREEN PEPPER, PARSLEY, PAPRIKA, CAYENNE AND ALL OF THE LEMON JUICE OVER OYSTERS. PLACE REMAINING OYSTERS AND SEASONING ON TOP. SPRINKLE WITH CREAM AND BUTTER BITS. ROLL BISCUIT DOUGH THIN. CUT OUT CENTERS LIKE DOUGHNUTS. PUT ON PIE.

BAKE AT 400° FOR 20 MINUTES

Serves 4, or Chick and one other as a main course.

EVY'S SCALLOPED OYSTERS

2 C. COARSELY CRUSHED SALTINE CRACKERS
½ C. MELTED BUTTER
1 QT. OYSTERS
1 C. HEAVY CREAM
SALT, CAYENNE PEPPER TO TASTE

IN A BUTTERED CASSEROLE LAYER ⅓ CRUMBS, ½ OF THE OYSTERS, ⅓ CRUMBS. RESERVE ¼ C. OYSTER LIQUID. ADD LIQUID TO THE HEAVY CREAM, SALT AND CAYENNE PEPPER. POUR REMAINING OYSTERS AND LIQUID OVER CASSEROLE, TOP WITH REMAINING CRUMBS.

BAKE 15-20 MINUTES AT 400°

Chick's at the oven door waiting for this dish to finish every time. Our best advice about this dish is-
double the amount to serve more than four

SHRIMP AND FISH SCAMPI

1   LB. SHRIMP, PEELED
1   LB. FISH, OF CHOICE CUT IN BITE SIZE PIECES
3   CLOVES OF GARLIC, CHOPPED
4   TBS. FRESH PARSLEY
½   LEMON OR LIME
½   C. OLIVE OIL

IN A BROILER PAN HEAT OIL, BUTTER, GARLIC. ADD
SHRIMP AND FISH IN A SINGLE LAYER. SQUEEZE
LEMON/LIME JUICE OVER LAYER. BROIL UNTIL FIRM.
TRANSFER TO A HEATED PLATTER. SPRINKLE WITH
PARSLEY. POUR SAUCE FROM PAN ONTO DISH.

*Grandpa likes his served with gnocchi and crusty
bread. Buy gnocchi (Italian potato dumplings) in the
frozen food section. Serve a platter of antipasto as
a first course for an easy "company dinner." All
darlings love Italian.*

BAKED FISH

WHAT CAN BE EASIER THAN PUTTING PIECES OF
FISH IN AN OVEN PAN, A PIECE OF BUTTER ON EACH
PIECE, A SQUEEZE OF LEMON OR LIME ON EACH
PIECE, AND BAKING AT 350° FOR ABOUT 10 MINUTES
TO THE INCH?

*A smart teen whose turn it was to cook answered
"going out to eat." Sometimes it's best to just
ignore them.*

TEMPURA BATTER FOR SEAFOOD

2   **EGG WHITES, SLIGHTLY BEATEN**
¾   **C. ICE WATER**
⅓   **C. CORNSTARCH**
⅔   **C. FLOUR**
½   **TSP. SALT**
      PEANUT OIL

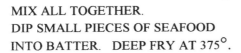

MIX ALL TOGETHER.
DIP SMALL PIECES OF SEAFOOD
INTO BATTER. DEEP FRY AT 375°.

*The batter can also be used to fry vegetables. Be sure
to reveal that this style of cooking is Japanese. Info
about cultural diversity can be filling. Give them
many helpings.*

FRIED OYSTERS

1   **PINT OYSTERS**
1   **EGG, BEATEN**
1½   **C. CRACKER MEAL**
      PEANUT OIL

DRAIN OYSTERS DIP INDIVIDUALLY INTO EGG THEN
INTO CRACKER MEAL. ONCE IS ENOUGH.
FRY IN A SINGLE LAYER OF ½" OIL AT CONSTANT
375° TEMPERATURE UNTIL GOLDEN. TURN ONCE.
DO NOT OVERCOOK.
USE TWO PANS IF NECESSARY.

Serve with cocktail sauce

BEFORE SPANISH RICE

Leave the cooking to the kids occasionally. If they can read, they can cook. So the kitchen is destroyed in the process--it might be worth the trauma to launch a future chef. All you need to get started on this wonderful learning experience is a tried and true recipe.

Think of the confidence it will instill in your "little darling": one need not be reduced to starvation without Mom at home or a T.V. dinner in the freezer. Hand the kid the recipe and leave.

Only a doting grandmother would be brave enough to stick around for the agony to follow.

SPICY SPANISH RICE WITH TUNA

¼	C. OIL
1	C. RICE
1	GREEN PEPPER, CHOPPED
1	TSP. SALT
1	CLOVE GARLIC
1	10 OZ. CAN TOMATOES AND GREEN CHILIS
1	CAN MUSHROOMS
1	C. WATER
1	7 OZ. CAN TUNA

HEAT OIL IN LARGE SKILLET ADD RICE AND COOK TO GOLDEN COLOR. ADD REMAINING INGREDIENTS, EXCEPT TUNA. COVER COOK OVER LOW HEAT 35 MINUTES OR UNTIL RICE IS DONE, STIRRING OCCASIONALLY.
ADD TUNA, HEAT THROUGH.

SHRIMP and GRAPEFRUIT SALAD

2   **C. LETTUCE, SHREDDED**
½   **TO 1 POUND COOKED SHRIMP**
1   **SMALL ONION, MINCED**
1   **C. RADISHES, SLICED VERY THIN**
½   **C. CELERY, SLICED**
1   **C. BLACK EYE PEAS COOKED, WASHED AND DRAINED**
1   **RED GRAPEFRUIT, CUT IN SECTIONS**

TOSS ONION WITH PEAS. COVER 13" PLATTER WITH LETTUCE. MOUND PEAS IN THE CENTER. DISTRIBUTE SLICED VEGETABLES AROUND PEAS. ALTERNATE SHRIMP AND GRAPEFRUIT SECTIONS ALONG EDGE OF PLATTER.

DRESSING for SHRIMP SALAD

½   **C. OLIVE OIL**
¼   **C. RICE VINEGAR**
2   **TBS. GRAPEFRUIT JUICE**
¼   **TSP. SALT**
     PEPPER IF DESIRED

SWEET AND SOUR SAUCE FOR WHAT'S ON SALE

All sized darlings will happily consume your choice of fish, shrimp, scallops, or meat if they can dip it in this sauce. Liver is the exception although the cat will think it palatable.

1   C. SUGAR
½   C. CIDER VINEGAR
1   TBS. GREEN PEPPER, CHOPPED FINE
1   TBS. RED PEPPER, CHOPPED FINE
1   TSP. PAPRIKA
¼   TSP. SALT
2   TSP. CORNSTARCH, MIXED WITH
      1 TBS. COLD WATER

COMBINE ALL EXCEPT CORNSTARCH MIXTURE. COOK 15 MINUTES. ADD CORNSTARCH, STIRRING UNTIL THICK.

Saute, fry, bake, or broil depending on your choice of entree. Little ones do like small cubed pieces. Chick likes pork tenderloins roasted, sliced, and drowned in this sauce. Serve with rice.

36

SHRIMP CREOLE

1   **LB. SHRIMP, PEELED AND DEVEINED**
1   **14 ½ OZ. CAN TOMATOES**
1   **8 OZ. CAN TOMATO SAUCE**
6   **STRIPS BACON**
1   **TBS. WORCESTERSHIRE SAUCE**
1   **TBS. CREOLE SEASONING BLEND**
1   **ONION, CHOPPED**
1   **MED. GREEN PEPPER, CHOPPED**
1   **MED. RED PEPPER, CHOPPED**

FRY BACON; DRAIN ON PAPER TOWELS. DRAIN OFF
AS MUCH GREASE AS POSSIBLE FROM PAN. LEAVE
CRUMBS IN PAN. IN SAME PAN, SAUTE ONIONS AND
PEPPERS UNTIL SOFT. ADD TOMATOES AND TOMATO
SAUCE. HEAT THOROUGHLY. ADD SHRIMP AND
SIMMER 20 MIN. STIR IN WORCESTERSHIRE.
CRUMBLE BACON OVER CREOLE.

SERVE OVER RICE OR PASTA

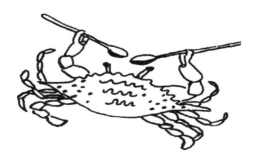

37

FISHERMEN'S PORT CHOWDER

1 LB. FISH OF CHOICE, CUT IN BITE SIZE PIECES
½ LB. BAY SCALLOPS
1 MED. TURNIP, CHOPPED
1 LARGE CARROT, SLICED
1 MED. ONION, CHOPPED
1 C. CELERY, SLICED
2 C. RAW POTATOES, CUBED
3 CLOVES GARLIC, CRUSHED
1 14 ½ OZ. CAN TOMATOES, CHOPPED
1½ C. CHICKEN BROTH or FISH STOCK
1 8 OZ. BOTTLE CLAM JUICE
1 C. DRY WHITE WINE
½ TSP. THYME
1 TSP. MARJORAM
2 TBS. OLIVE OIL

SAUTE VEGETABLES IN OIL TO BLEND FLAVOR. ADD
TOMATOES, CHICKEN BROTH, CLAM JUICE, AND WINE.
COOK 25 MINUTES. ADD SEAFOOD, THYME, AND
MARJORAM. COVER, COOK 20 MINUTES. SERVE IN
WARMED BOWLS.

*"Little darlings," need not know how fish stock is
made. All good cooks have their secrets. Its O.K.
Lots of info is on a need to know basis for kids.*

SHRIMP BURGERS

1½   **LB. SHRIMP, COOKED, CHOPPED**
½   **C. CELERY, CHOPPED**
1   **SMALL ONION, CHOPPED**
8   **OZ. CAN WATER CHESTNUTS, CHOPPED COARSELY**
2   **EGGS**
¼   **C. MAYONNAISE**
1   **TBS. PARSLEY**
2   **C. BREAD CRUMBS**
8   **SLICES MILD WHITE HAVARTI CHEESE**
8   **BUNS**

BLEND ALL EXCEPT CRUMBS AND CHEESE.
FORM INTO PATTIES. COVER WITH CRUMBS.
FRY TO GOLDEN BROWN, TURNING ONCE.
DO NOT CROWD IN PAN.

Place cheese slice on warmed buns. Add burgers; pass the tartar sauce.

FLORIDA FESTIVE GROUPER

1 **TO 2 POUNDS GROUPER FILLETS**
¼ **C. OLIVE OIL AND 1 TBS. BUTTER, MIXED**
2 **CLOVES GARLIC, SLICED**
1 **GREEN PEPPER, CUT IN THIN STRIPS**
1 **YELLOW PEPPER, CUT IN THIN STRIPS**
1 **RED PEPPER, CUT IN THIN STRIPS**
1 **MEDIUM ONION, SLICED**
1 **C. OLIVES WITH PIMIENTO**
1 **LEMON**
2 **TOMATOES, SEEDED AND CHOPPED**
1 **C. DRY WHITE WINE**
2 **BAY LEAVES**
1 **TSP. PAPRIKA**

LIGHTLY SAUTE PEPPERS, ONION, AND GARLIC IN OIL
AND BUTTER. SQUEEZE LEMON OVER PAN. ADD OLIVES,
CHOPPED TOMATOES, WINE, BAY LEAVES, PAPRIKA,
STIRRING TO REDUCE LIQUID SLIGHTLY.
POUR OVER FISH IN A BUTTERED DISH COVER.
BAKE 350° UNTIL FISH FLAKES EASILY.

*A very pretty dish and oh, so tasty. Chick likes
it so much he doesn't want to wait for festive occasions.*

40

FISH STUFFED
with CRABMEAT

1 **POUND CRAB MEAT**
2 **TBS. ONION, MINCED**
¼ **C. CELERY, MINCED**
¼ **C. MAYONNAISE**
1 **TSP. CATSUP**
2 **SLICES BACON**
3 **TO 5 POUND WHOLE FISH WITH HEAD ON** *

WASH FISH IN COLD WATER.
PAT DRY WITH PAPER TOWEL.

MIX CRAB MEAT WITH ONION, CELERY, MAYONNAISE
AND CATSUP. STUFF FISH CAVITY. PLACE BACON
THE LENGTH OF FISH. ADD A LITTLE WATER TO PAN.
COVER. BAKE 350°. TEST IN 20 MINUTES. COOK
UNTIL FISH FLAKES EASILY. FINISH UNCOVERED TO
BROWN BACON.

*Need not tell you how many interesting comments
you can expect from the "fish stick crowd" about
the fish's head being left on when served.*

*
*Try Red Snapper or a "little darlings" own catch.
If no catch is caught, crab cakes sound good. Add an
egg to stuffing and a few bread crumbs, and saute
away. There is always another fishing day.*

SCALLOPS and PASTA SHELLS

1   LB. SCALLOPS. IF LARGE, CUT INTO 4 PIECES
3   TBS. OLIVE OIL
2   TBS. BUTTER
3   CLOVES GARLIC, SLICED
2   TBS. PARSLEY, DRIED
    SALT AND PEPPER TO TASTE
½   LB. PASTA, SHELL SHAPE
    PARMESAN CHEESE

SAUTE SCALLOPS AND GARLIC IN BLENDED OIL
AND BUTTER. ADD PARSLEY. POUR OVER COOKED
PASTA. TOSS. SERVE IN WARMED DISH. GARNISH
WITH CHEESE.

This entree can be stretched like a rubber band
if you give in to that often heard plea, "Can I ask
_____ to eat with us?" You fill in the blank and
add more seafood and a vegetable.

SHRIMP RAREBIT

½ **TO 1 POUND COOKED SHRIMP, CHOPPED**
3 **TBS. BUTTER**
3 **TBS. FLOUR**
½ **POUND SHARP NATURAL CHEDDAR CHEESE,**
  GRATED
1½ **C. MILK**

MELT BUTTER. ADD FLOUR, STIRRING UNTIL
ABSORBED. ADD MILK AND CHEESE, STIRRING
UNTIL THICKENED. ADD SEASONINGS AND
CHOPPED SHRIMP. SERVE ON TOAST ON WARMED
PLATES.

TUNA A-LA-KING

1 **CAN TUNA, WELL DRAINED**
1 **STALK CELERY, SLICED**
1 **SMALL ONION**
1 **TB. GREEN PEPPER, CHOPPED**
1 **2 OZ. JAR DRIED PIMIENTOS**
2 **TBS. BUTTER OR OLIVE OIL**
1 **C. MILK**
2 **TBS. FLOUR**

SAUTE VEGETABLES IN BUTTER. ADD 2 TBS. FLOUR
AND 1 C. MILK, STIRRING UNTIL THICKENED. ADD
TUNA AND PIMIENTOS.

*Serve on toast, waffles, noodles, baked potato, or in
pastry cup. Chopped ham, chicken or seafood
may be substituted.*

CLASSIC TARTAR SAUCE

From 1927 recipe book by U.S. Fisheries Association

1 C. MAYO
1 TBS. MINCED PARSLEY
1 TBS. MINCED ONION
1 TBS. CAPERS
1 TBS. MINCED PICKLE OR OLIVE

MIX----CHILL. JUICE OF LEMON OR LIME IS OPTIONAL

COCKTAIL SAUCE

½ C. CHILI SAUCE (NOT CATSUP)
1 TSP. HORSERADISH
LEMON/LIME TO TASTE

Best known by little darlings as "that red stuff" and by Grandpa as "red sauce."

CUCUMBER SAUCE

1 SMALL CUCUMBER PEEL, SEED, CHOP FINE
1 TBS. MINCED ONION
SALT AND PEPPER
1 C. SOUR CREAM OR YOGURT
1 TSP. DILL

CHOP CUCUMBER FINE. DRAIN ON PAPER TOWEL.
ADD WITH ONION TO SOUR CREAM. SALT, PEPPER
TO TASTE.

LEMON LIME BUTTER SAUCE

**TO MELTED BUTTER, ADD LEMON OR LIME
JUICE TO TASTE -----------ADD PARSLEY**

*Put into a sauce boat that fits over a warming candle.
"Little darlings" are intrigued by candle light.*

LEMON BARBEQUE SAUCE

½   **CUP FRESH LEMON JUICE**
½   **CUP SALAD OIL**
1½   **TSP. BLACK PEPPER**
2   **TSP. GRATED ONION**
1   **TSP. DRY MUSTARD**
2   **TSP. BROWN SUGAR**
½   **TSP. SALT**

MIX INGREDIENTS WELL STIRRING UNTIL SUGAR
IS DISSOLVED. BASTE FISH FREQUENTLY
WITH SAUCE.

CHILI CRAB CRUSTLESS QUICHE

1¼	LB. MUENSTER CHEESE, GRATED
6	OZ. CAN CRAB MEAT, RINSED AND WELL DRAINED
4.5	OZ. CAN CHOPPED CHILIS
6	EGGS, BEATEN
12	SODA CRACKERS, CRUSHED
1	C. HALF AND HALF SOURED WITH 1 TSP. VINEGAR
½	TSP. SEAFOOD SEASONING PAPRIKA TO TASTE

MIX ALL INGREDIENTS. PUT IN AN OILED 11"X 13" PAN. SPRINKLE TOP WITH PAPRIKA. BAKE 325° UNTIL LIGHTLY BROWNED AND FIRM, ABOUT 45 MINUTES.

FRUITS *and*
VEGETABLES

Raw is easy:

We were delighted when we observed that vegetables "our darlings" did not like cooked were eaten ravenously when presented raw. Like most phases, it didn't last long even though we never let slip that raw was most nutritious.

Tossed:

Salads are popular courses with "teen darlings" watching their weight for many reasons, including maintaining wrestling weight. Coaches can be an ally in the quest to advance healthy eating. We did not add a huge variety of vegetables to our tossed salad or we had several "little darlings" doing scientific examinations among the greens to see if there was some item they considered "ugh." We all like to be able to identify what we are eating.

Cooked:

"Don't kill them", profound directions by a friend from the Orient. Overcooked is bad.

Leftovers:

"Little darlings" like them best marinated, tossed with pasta or folded in macaroni and cheese.

BAKED RUSSET POTATOES

MEDIUM POTATOES
SCRUB WITH VEGETABLE BRUSH AND DRY
OIL LIGHTLY TO KEEP THE SKIN SOFT

BAKE ABOUT AN HOUR AT 350°

*The choice of a busy teen darling whose cooking creed is "**Simplification.**"*

*Then there is "**fancy**" meal preparation practiced by an engaged darling to impress the future spouse.*

SCALLOPED
RED POTATOES made FANCY

8 **MEDIUM POTATOES, UNPEELED**
1½ **C. LEEKS, SLICED THIN**
½ **C. BACON CRUMBS**
1 **C. RAW PEAS**
3 **EGGS, HARD BOILED**
1 **C. CREAM**
3 **TBS. FLOUR**
4 **TSP. BUTTER**
½ **C. CHEDDAR CHEESE**

Boil potatoes to just done, cut ¼" slices. Fry bacon, drain and crumble. Butter 1 qt. casserole. Layer ¼" potato slices, a few leeks and half of bacon, more potatoes. sliced eggs, potatoes, bacon, peas and cheddar, ending with layer of potatoes. Mix flour and cream, pour over casserole, add 4 pats of butter, cover. Bake at 350° 40 minutes. Uncover, bake 15 minutes more.

SWEET POTATO BAKE

- **3**   **LBS. SWEET POTATOES, MASHED**
- **½**   **STICK OF BUTTER**
- **2**   **TBS. BROWN SUGAR, OPTIONAL**
- **½**   **TSP. SALT**
- **1**   **TSP. VANILLA**
- **2**   **TSP. ORANGE RIND**
- **½**   **CUP ORANGE JUICE**

COMBINE ALL INGREDIENTS.
SPOON INTO A GREASED BAKING DISH.
BAKE 30 MINUTES AT 350°.

DOWN ON THE FARM

Just about every meal had potatoes. Now we use a greater variety of starches, as many as our hips can afford, but "little darlings" love mashed potatoes best of all.

INSTANT WHITE POTATOES

SUBSTITUTE SOUR CREAM FOR ½ C. OF THE LIQUID USED TO MAKE INSTANT POTATOES ADD BUTTER AND PARSLEY FLAKES. GRANDMA LIKES GARLIC SALT AND CHIVES.

GRANDPA MAKES MASHED POTATO SALAD BY ADDING RAW MINCED ONION, CELERY AND SWEET PICKLE.

50

BARLEY-MUSHROOM PILAF

2	TBS. BUTTER OR OLIVE OIL
1	CUP SLICED MUSHROOMS
1	CUP CHOPPED ONIONS
1	CUP MEDIUM PEARL BARLEY
¼	CUP CHOPPED GREEN PEPPER
2	CUPS CHICKEN BROTH
½	TSP. SALT, DASH PEPPER
¼	CUP CHOPPED PARSLEY

MELT BUTTER IN 3 QUART SAUCEPAN. SAUTE
MUSHROOMS, ONION, AND GREEN PEPPER. ADD
BARLEY, BROTH, SALT AND PEPPER. STIR, BRING
TO BOIL. REDUCE HEAT; COVER AND SIMMER
UNTIL BARLEY IS TENDER AND LIQUID IS GONE,
ABOUT 25 MINUTES.
STIR IN PARSLEY.

*The "little darlings" are going
to have a learning experience
when they pipe up with
"what's this stuff?"
We leave it to you to explain.
This dish is a nice change from
potatoes or rice.*

51

MIXED VEGETABLE CASSEROLE

1 LB. FRESH GREEN BEANS
½ LB. FRESH YELLOW BEANS
2 LARGE TOMATOES CUT ¼ INCH THICK
½ TSP. SALT
½ TSP. PEPPER
2 LARGE CARROTS, THINLY SLICED
1 LARGE GREEN PEPPER, CUT IN 1 INCH SQUARES
2 RIBS OF CELERY, SLICED
10 SMALL WHITE ONIONS
¼ CUP OF MINCED SCALLIONS
¼ CUP PARSLEY
1 TSP. BASIL
½ TSP. THYME
¼ CUP OLIVE OIL
¼ CUP DRY WHITE WINE OR BOUILLON

SLIGHTLY PARBOIL OR STEAM BEANS. IN A 2½ QUART CASSEROLE PUT GREEN AND YELLOW BEANS AROUND OUTER SIDES OF THE DISH. CAREFULLY LAYER OTHER VEGETABLES IN THE CENTER. PUT SCALLIONS, PARSLEY, BASIL AND THYME ON TOP.

BLEND OIL AND WINE AND POUR OVER VEGETABLES

COVER AND BAKE 40 MINUTES AT 350°

52

SMOKY STRING BEANS
and NEW POTATOES

2 **LB. FROZEN CUT GREEN BEANS**
2 **LB. SMALL NEW POTATOES, UNPEELED**
1 **TBS. BUTTER**
1 **TBS. LIQUID SMOKE**
2 **TSP. DRIED ONION FLAKES**
1 **CAN CHICKEN BRPTH OPTIONAL**

COVER BEANS WITH WATER OR CHICKEN BROTH
IN A PAN LARGE ENOUGH FOR BOTH VEGETABLES.
BOIL 10 MIN., LOWER HEAT, STIR IN SMOKE, ONIONS
AND BUTTER. LAYER POTATOES ON TOP OF BEANS,
COVER AND COOK UNTIL POTATOES ARE TENDER.

*Grandpa said he liked to start beans with a big piece
of fat back , cubed and fried in the pan. Older
"darlings" were aghast! Little one didn't get it.*
*This kind of family information is a matter of
historical or hysterical interest depending on your
cholesterol level.*

TEN GOLDEN CORN CAKES

1½ **C. CORN, FRESH, CANNED OR FROZEN**
 ½ **C. CELERY, CHOPPED**
2   **EGGS, BEATEN**
 ½ **C. BISCUIT MIX**
 ½ **C. PARMESAN CHEESE**

MIX ALL INGREDIENTS . BATTER WILL BE STIFF.
USING SOUP SPOON SPREAD EACH SPOONFUL ONTO
A GREASED GRIDDLE OR PAN. FRY UNTIL GOLDEN.

53

YELLOW SQUASH CASSEROLE

A troops bumper crop of squash

4   **LB. YELLOW SQUASH, GRATED**
1   **MED. CHOPPED ONION**
4   **TBS. BUTTER**
1   **CAN MUSHROOM SOUP, UNDILUTED**
1   **C. GRATED CHEDDAR CHEESE**

BOIL SQUASH AND ONION UNTIL TENDER.
ADD BUTTER AND SOUP. PUT INTO OVEN
CASSEROLE. COVER WITH CHEESE.

BAKE 350° UNTIL BUBBLY HOT AND CHEESE
IS MELTED.

*It's amazing how easy it is to grow squash.
Darling farmers either want to pick them before
ready or let them grow until they are huge
and tough.*

Take pictures of the harvest and the proud farmers.

MARMALADE CARROTS

2½   **C. CARROTS, SLICED THIN, COOKED**
1   **TBS. BUTTER**
¼   **C. ORANGE OR LIME OR LEMON MARMALADE**
1   **TSP. FRESH ORANGE, LIME OR LEMON JUICE**
¼   **TSP. GINGER**

MELT BUTTER. ADD ALL INGREDIENTS. BLEND
AND HEAT UNTIL SMOOTH. TOSS WITH CARROTS.

54

STUFFED ACORN SQUASH

½ SQUASH FOR EACH DINER
ITALIAN SAUSAGE, COOKED AND CRUMBLED
ZUCCHINI, TOMATOES AND ONION CHOPPED.
MOZZARELLA CHEESE, SLICED.

CUT SQUASH LENGTHWISE. PLACE CUT SIDE
SIDE DOWN IN PAN, COVERING THE BOTTOM WITH ½
INCH OF WATER OR BROTH. BAKE 350° UNTIL TENDER.
DRAIN ON PAPER TOWELS. SAUTE VEGETABLES; ADD
SAUSAGE. MOUND INTO SQUASH SHELLS. TOP WITH
MOZZARELLA AND BROIL UNTIL CHEESE IS MELTED.
ONE POUND of SAUSAGE AND 3 CUPS OF VEGETABLES
IS ENOUGH FOR 4 SQUASH. ADJUST AMOUNT OF
INGREDIENTS TO SIZE OF SQUASH.

CONVERT TO A GREAT VEGETARIAN MAIN DISH
BY OMITTING SAUSAGE AND ADDING A PASTA
OR WILD RICE.

*Darling home ec student announced we all
should have a yellow vegetable once a week.
We thought we had hidden it under the stuffing.
Little ones were confused. At times like these,
we just say "that's good" and change the topic
of conversation.*

55

RUTABAGA-LIMA BEAN TOSS

1   **RUTABAGA, DICED**
1   **PKG. FROZEN LIMA BEANS**
    COOK EACH VEGETABLE SEPARATELY
2   **TBS. MELTED BUTTER**
½   **TSP. POPPY SEED**

Combine all, tossing gently with butter and seeds.

ELEGANT EGGPLANT

1   **LARGE EGGPLANT, DICED**
1   **MED. YELLOW SQUASH, SLICED**
1   **PKG. SUGAR SNAP PEAS**
2   **CLOVES GARLIC**
1   **TSP. FINE HERBS**
½   **TSP. GROUND CUMIN**
    OLIVE OIL

HEAT OIL VERY HOT. SAUTE VEGETABLES WITH
CRUSHED GARLIC. SEASON WHEN VEGETABLES
ARE ALMOST DONE.

*The little darlings can't
quite figure out the
seasoning in this dish,
but they eat it "all gone."
They thrive on intrigue;
it expands their little
minds.*

VEGETABLE FEAST

BROCCOLI	**CARROTS**
CAULIFLOWER	**GREEN BEANS**
CABBAGE WEDGES	**BRUSSELS SPROUTS**
CHERRY TOMATOES	**TURNIP HALVES**
ZUCCHINI CHUNKS	**SNOW PEAS**
SMALL WHOLE ONIONS	

SMALL RED SKIN POTATOES, UNPEELED, WHOLE

Load up a steamer pan with your choice of at least 5 vegetables, including potatoes. Cook until done, but still firm.

Arrange on a small warmed platter. Serve with cheese sauce.

CHEESE SAUCE

2 **TBS. BUTTER**
2 **TBS. FLOUR**
1 **C. MILK**
1 **C. LONGHORN CHEESE, GRATED**
½ **TSP. PAPRIKA**

MELT BUTTER. BLEND IN FLOUR. ADD MILK, STIRRING UNTIL SAUCE THICKENS. REMOVE FROM HEAT. ADD CHEESE, PAPRIKA. MIX WELL. SERVE IN WARMED BOWLS.

ONE OR TWO FRESH CHOPPED HERBS ARE A NICE ACCOMPANIMENT.

SPINACH and ARTICHOKE HEART CASSEROLE

2 PKG. FROZEN CHOPPED SPINACH
1 14 OZ. CAN ARTICHOKE HEARTS, WATER PACKED
¼ LB. BUTTER
3 OZ. CREAM CHEESE
¼ C. MILK
1 C. BREAD CRUMBS, BUTTERED
   SALT, PEPPER TO TASTE

COOK SPINACH, DRAIN WELL SQUEEZING OUT LIQUID. CUT HEARTS IN HALF. MELT BUTTER. ADD CREAM CHEESE AND MILK BLENDING INTO A SMOOTH SAUCE.

LAYER ½ ARTICHOKES, SAUCE, SPINACH, FOLLOWED BY REMAINDER OF ARTICHOKES AND SAUCE. TOP WITH CRUMBS. BAKE 350° UNTIL HEATED THROUGH.

Cashew halves make an interesting garnish. A good company dish.

BROILED TOMATOES

CUT FULLY RIPE TOMATOES IN HALF, ½ TO 1 TOMATO PER PERSON. BROIL UNTIL BUBBLY BUT NOT COLLAPSED. SPRINKLE EACH WITH 1 TBS. PARMESAN CHEESE AND BROIL UNTIL CHEESE IS SLIGHTLY BROWNED.

One "darling" thought that tomatoes should only be served on fast food hamburgers until they tasted them broiled.

CARROT NUT LOAF

4   C, CARROTS, GRATED
1   8 OZ. PKG. HERB SEASONED STUFFING
1   LARGE ONION, CHOPPED
3   CLOVES GARLIC, MINCED
4   TBS. MELTED BUTTER
2   C. ENGLISH WALNUTS, CHOPPED FINE
1   C. VEGETABLE BROTH
4   EGGS, BEATEN
1   TSP. NUTMEG.

MIX ALL INGREDIENTS IN A LARGE BOWL.
PAT INTO AN OILED LOAF PAN. BAKE AT 350°
COVERED FOR 45 MINUTES. UNCOVER AND
CONTINUE TO BAKE UNTIL BROWNED. TO TEST
PIERCE LOAF WITH A WOODEN SKEWER. IF IT COMES
OUT CLEAN, LOAF IS DONE. LOOSEN, TURN ONTO
WARM PLATTER. COVER AND ALLOW TO SET 15
MINUTES BEFORE CUTTING.

*Pass the catsup and the "little darlings" might
think this is meat loaf.*

*For more sophisticated tastes we suggest the
following garnish:*

FRESH VEGETABLE SALSA

2   TOMATOES, SEEDED, CHOPPED
1   AVOCADO, CUBED
2   STALKS CELERY, SLICED THIN
1   SMALL CAN GREEN CHILIS
2   TSP. MILD VINEGAR
1   TSP. SUGAR

MIX. ALLOW FLAVORS TO BLEND AT ROOM
TEMPERATURE BEFORE SERVING.

COUNTRY COLE SLAW

1 **MED. CABBAGE, SHREDDED**
1 **TBS. SALT**
2 **MED. WHITE ONIONS, CHOPPED**
1 **GREEN PEPPER, CHOPPED**

COVER WITH COLD WATER TO TOP OF CHOPPED
VEGETABLES. REFRIGERATE TO CRISP.

DRESSING

½ **C. SUGAR**
½ **C. VINEGAR**
½ **TSP. SALT**
½ **TSP. DRY MUSTARD**
½ **C. OIL**

BOIL SUGAR, VINEGAR, SALT AND MUSTARD UNTIL
BLENDED. REMOVE FROM HEAT. COOL. BEAT IN OIL.
DRAIN VEGETABLES AND TOSS WITH DRESSING. CHILL
BEFORE SERVING. BEST MADE THE DAY BEFORE TO
BLEND FLAVORS.

SUMMER SLAW

Chick often gets real creative in the kitchen. Sometimes we eat his creations and sometimes we feed them to the chickens. This one we ate. It's different and we think you'll like its fresh taste with grilled meats.

2 **LARGE STALKS BOK CHOY, INCLUDING GREEN LEAVES**
2 **STALKS CELERY**
1 **MED. CUCUMBER, SEEDED**
4 **RED RADISHES**
½ **ONION**
   SALT AND PEPPER TO TASTE

CHOP ALL AS FOR COLE SLAW. A FOOD PROCESSOR MAKES IT EASY. IF YOU DON'T HAVE A PROCESSOR GET ONE. THE 'LITTLE DARLINGS' WILL BE GRATEFUL FOR THIS LESS WORK MACHINE.

TOSS WITH GOOD DRESSING.

GOOD DRESSING

⅓ **C. OIL**
1 **TBS. APPLE CIDER VINEGAR**
1 **TSP. SOY SAUCE**
½ **TSP. CELERY SEEDS**

BLEND WITH WIRE WHISK

GREEN AND WHITE
SUMMER SALAD

GREEN PEPPERS, THIN STRIPS
SWEET ONION, SMALL, SLICED
CELERY STALK, SLICED THIN
DAIKON RADISH, GRATED
SERVE ON A BED OF BOSTON LETTUCE
AND WATERCRESS

ONION SALAD

1 **MEDIUM WHITE ONION, SLICED THIN**
½ **C. OLIVE OIL**
¼ **C. WHITE WINE VINEGAR**
¼ **TSP. SALT**
½ **TSP. SUGAR**
1 **EGG, HARD BOILED, CHOPPED FINE**

CUT ONION VERTICALLY INTO PAPER THIN
SLICES. MARINATE SLICES IN OIL, VINEGAR,
SALT, AND SUGAR FOR SEVERAL HOURS.
ARRANGE SLICES ON LETTUCE AND GARNISH
WITH EGG. WHIP MARINATE FROM ONIONS
AND POUR A PORTION, TO TASTE, OVER SALAD.

SALAD SOUP

*Put left over **mixed vegetable salad** into beef*
or chicken broth to make salad soup. Add to soup
from those little covered·dishes that migrate to the
rear of the refrigerator. A cup can re-energize a
"darling" after a hard, hard day at school which
has left them weak from overwork and barely able to
utter "I'm starving!"

SUCCOTASH SALAD

MARINATE COOKED LIMAS AND CORN IN
ITALIAN DRESSING. ADD SLICED STUFFED
OLIVES AND SPRINKLE WITH PARMESAN
CHEESE.

GREEN PEAS, SWEET POTATOES
and
MUSHROOM SALAD

MARINATE COOKED GREEN PEAS WITH A SMALL
AMOUNT OF CHOPPED ONION IN A FAVORITE
DRESSING. PUT ON A BED OF RED LETTUCE.
GARNISH WITH SLICED RAW MUSHROOMS AND
GRATED RAW SWEET POTATOES.

*Put grated sweet potatoes into a mild solution of
water with lemon juice to keep color fresh. Drain
on paper towel.*

GARDEN PLATE

ALTERNATE SLICES OF TOMATOES, ONIONS AND
CUCUMBER ON A CHILLED PLATTER. DOT SALAD
WITH MAYONNAISE. SPRINKLE
WITH DILL WEED.
SIMPLY THE BEST,
WHEN TOMATOES
ARE AT THEIR
PEAK.

CITRUS FRENCH
SALAD DRESSING

2 C. OLIVE OIL
1½ LEMONS, JUICED
1½ ORANGES, JUICED
½ C. TARRAGON VINEGAR
½ TBS. WORCESTERSHIRE SAUCE
1½ TSP. DRY MUSTARD
2 TSP. PAPRIKA
½ TSP. SALT
½ C. SUGAR
1 CLOVE OF GARLIC
½ C. CATSUP

Blend well. Will keep a long time in the refrigerator in a glass jar.

EASY THOUSAND ISLAND
DRESSING

1½ C. MAYONNAISE
¼ C. CHILI SAUCE
2 TBS. PICKLE RELISH
1 EGG. HARD BOILED, CHOPPED FINE

MIX AND CHILL.

Serve on wedges of iceburg lettuce or thick slices of Romaine. A necessity for Reuben sandwiches.

ALL AMERICAN SALAD DRESSING

1½ C. MAYONNAISE
⅓   C. NON DAIRY CREAMER
2   TBS. VINEGAR (MAY BE ADJUSTED TO
    YOUR TASTE)
1   TBS. LEMON JUICE
1   TBS. PARSLEY FLAKES
¼   TSP. EACH OF ONION POWDER,
    DILL WEED, PAPRIKA, CELERY SEED,
    SALT, BLACK PEPPER.
1   TBS. SUGAR, OPTIONAL

DEEEEELLICIOUS

*We seldom buy salad dressing at the store.
Most of those expensive little bottles taste
to us like total chemical composition. Many
seem to have a consistency near glue.
We have tried to devise a salad dressing using
seasonings we keep on hand. This recipe
takes 5 minutes and makes 16 ounces.*

ORANGE PINEAPPLE RICE

1   **C. RICE**
2   **C. ORANGE JUICE**
1   **SMALL CAN PINEAPPLE CHUNKS**
1   **MED. RED APPLE, CHOPPED**
½ **C. CELERY, CHOPPED FINE**
¼ **C. PECANS, CHOPPED**
1   **TSP. ORANGE RIND, OPTIONAL**
2   **TBS. BUTTER**

SAUTE CELERY AND PECANS. REMOVE FROM PAN. ADD RICE AND ORANGE JUICE. WHILE RICE IS COOKING, CHOP APPLE AND CUT EACH PINEAPPLE CHUNK IN 3 PIECES. WHEN RICE IS COOKED, ADD FRUIT AND NUTS. MIX. SERVE WARM.

Grandpa loves it with ham or chicken.

PEACH HALVES in RED* GELATIN

1   **C. LETTUCE, SHREDDED**
1   **CAN PEACH HALVES, DRAINED**
1   **PKG. RED GELATIN**

DRAIN PEACH HALVES. MIX GELATIN. ADD A PEACH HALF FOR EACH DINER. REFRIGERATE UNTIL FIRM. PLACE EACH SERVING ON A BED OF LETTUCE.

If used as a dessert omit lettuce, top each serving with whipped cream.

WHIPPING CREAM

WHIP CREAM WITH 2 TSP. POWDERED SUGAR AND A TSP. OF VANILLA.

* *It has to be red. No substitutes are acceptable.*
You can't mess with a childhood classic.

POLKA DOT RICE

1 **C. RICE**
2 **C. BROTH OR WATER**
2 **TBS. BUTTER**
2 **TSP. CURRY POWDER**
1 **TOMATO, SEEDED AND DICED**
½ **C. GREEN PEAS**
¼ **C. ONION, MINCED**
¼ **C. BLACK OLIVES, CHOPPED**

COOK RICE IN BROTH. WHILE STILL HOT,
FLUFF WITH BUTTER AND CURRY POWDER
TO MAKE A BEAUTIFUL GOLD COLOR.

MIX IN OTHER INGREDIENTS.

SERVES 4

SKEWERED FRUIT

AN ASSORTMENT OF FRESH FRUIT OF CHOICE
AND MEDIUM WOODEN SKEWERS, GREEN AND
RED MARASCHINO CHERRIES WITH STEMS.
HELPERS WITH CLEAN HANDS.

THREAD CHUNKS OF FRUIT ONTO SKEWERS,
STARTING AND ENDING WITH GREEN AND RED
CHERRIES. ARRANGE ON A PRETTY PLATTER.

DIP FOR FRUIT

1	**C. VANILLA YOGURT**
¼	**C. CHOPPED NUTS**

FRUIT CUP

4	**ORANGES, PEELED AND SECTIONS REMOVED**
1	**APPLE, UNPEELED, CHOPPED**
1	**SMALL CAN CRUSHED PINEAPPLE**
1	**KIWI, SLICED. CUT EACH SLICE INTO 4 PIECES**

MACAROONS, ONE FOR EACH SERVING.

MIX FRUIT. GARNISH EACH SERVING WITH A
CRUMBLED MACAROON.
Adult serving can be splashed with Cointreau.

WATER MELON BALLS IN GINGER ALE

1   **WATER MELON, CUT LENGTHWISE**
1   **OR 2 FRUIT BALL SCOOPS: FRIENDS WITH**
    SCOOPS ARE WELCOME.
1   **CAN OF GINGER ALE**
2   **PLASTIC BOWLS, ONE FOR BALLS, ONE FOR**
    SCRAPS. A WORK TABLE OUTDOORS.

POUT GINGER ALE OVER THE BALLS IN THE
BOWL. REFRIGERATE.

*Grandpa almost ran the lawnmower over his
foot watching the activity. He gave up on the lawn,
joined in eating left overs, and finally got the hose
for cleanup.*

MARSHMALLOW PINEAPPLE RINGS

PINEAPPLE RINGS
BROWN SUGAR
MINIATURE MARSHMALLOWS

DRAIN RINGS. SPRINKLE WITH BROWN SUGAR.
DOT EACH RING WITH 6 MARSHMALLOWS. BROIL.

*Smallest "little darlings" idea of fancy fare. Almost
as popular as canned peach halves in red gelatin,
topped with a big spoon full of whipped cream.*

*The words whipped cream and epicurean are
synonymous to the "little darlings."*

CHOCOLATE PEARS

BOSC PEARS, ONE PER DINER.
BOTTLE OF CHOCOLATE SHELL TOPPING.
SLICED ALMONDS FOR GARNISH.

DO NOT PEEL PEARS, LEAVE STEM ATTACHED.
CUT A SLICE FROM THE BOTTOM OF THE PEARS
SO THEY WILL SIT UPRIGHT.

STEAM PEARS UNTIL FORK TENDER. DRAIN ON
PAPER TOWELS. CHILL IN FREEZER UNTIL VERY
COLD. TO SERVE, COAT WITH THE SHELL TOPPING
GARNISH.

*Watch "darling" eyes enlarge when given a fruit
knife and dessert fork. Home is the training ground.
We are the trainers.*

PEAR SAUCE

2   1 LB. CANS OF PEARS IN LIGHT SYRUP
3   MED. SLICES CANDIED GINGER

DRAIN PEARS, RESERVING 1 CUP TO CHOP
COARSELY. PUREE REMAINING PEARS. MINCE
GINGER, COMBINE WITH CHUNKS AND PUREE.

GOODIES

CHOCOLATE SHEET CAKE

Beloved by all and so easy to make that volunteers show up at the kitchen door. Leave in its pan for easy traveling to the spot where a "darling" volunteered you to deliver a treat. Makes 24 servings.

2	**C. FLOUR**
2	**C. SUGAR**
4	**TBS. COCOA**
1	**C. WATER**
1	**TSP. VANILLA**
1	**TSP. BAKING SODA**
¼	**LB. BUTTER**
½	**C. OIL**
¼	**TSP. SALT**
½	**C. SOUR MILK**
2	**EGGS**

IN A LARGE BOWL MIX FLOUR AND SUGAR. BRING TO A BOIL THE BUTTER, OIL, WATER AND COCOA. POUR HOT MIXTURE OVER FLOUR AND SUGAR. STIR UNTIL SMOOTH. BEAT EGGS, SOUR MILK, VANILLA, SALT AND SODA TOGETHER. ADD TO DOUGH. MIXING WELL. POUR INTO 11"X 15" SHEET CAKE PAN THAT HAS BEEN OILED AND FLOURED.

BAKE 400° 15 MINUTES.

FROSTING
FOR CHOCOLATE SHEET CAKE

¼ **LB. BUTTER**
5 **TBS. MILK**
4 **TBS. COCOA**
1 **LB. POWDERED SUGAR**
½ **TSP. VANILLA**

MELT BUTTER WITH MILK AND COCOA.
REMOVE FROM STOVE. ADD VANILLA AND
SUGAR. BEAT UNTIL SMOOTH.
SPREAD ON HOT CAKE.

TEACHER'S PET CHOCOLATE FUDGE

IN A LARGE METAL BOWL MIX

1   LB. LITTLE MARSHMALLOWS
18   OZ. CHOCOLATE CHIPS
2   TBS. BUTTER

BLEND IN SAUCEPAN

4½   C. SUGAR
1   12 OZ. CAN EVAPORATED MILK

BRING MILK AND SUGAR TO A ROLLING BOIL,
STIRRING CONSTANTLY. REDUCE HEAT AND BOIL
MIXTURE 15 MINUTES OR TO A SOFT BALL STAGE,
236°.
ADD

1   TBS. VANILLA

POUR HOT SUGAR-MILK OVER CHIPS AND
MARSHMALLOWS . BEAT UNTIL MELTED AND
SMOOTH. ADD:

2   C.   CHOPPED NUTS

POUR INTO BUTTERED SHEET PAN. MAKES 5 LBS.

*After school starts, in classrooms all over the land,
little hands are raised to volunteer us as room mothers
and fathers.*

*Nevertheless, not knowing that we had even applied
for the job, we usually sigh and bow to our fate.*

*We, the overworked, need all the help we can get
in keeping the treats supplied.*

74

CHOCOLATE WAFFLES

½ C. OIL
¾ C. SUGAR
2 EGGS, BEATEN
⅓ C. COCOA
1¼ C. FLOUR
1 TSP. BAKING POWDER
½ TSP. CINNAMON
½ TSP. SALT
½ C. MILK
1 TSP. VANILLA

MIX OIL AND SUGAR. ADD REMAINING INGREDIENTS.
SERVE WARM, TOPPED WITH ICE CREAM.

*There were lots of turned up noses when we
announced waffles for dessert until the "little
darlings" found out they were chocolate waffles.
A good lesson in being open minded.*

PEACH ICE CREAM

⅔ C. EAGLE BRAND SWEETENED MILK
½ C. WATER
1 C. CRUSHED PEACHES
¼ C. POWDERED SUGAR
1 C. WHIPPING CREAM

*We prepare the peaches but allow a "darling" to
put all the ingredients in an ice cream machine
and turn the handle for 20 minutes. Enough for
three "little darlings." Double if necessary.*

POUND CAKE
and 3 variations

½ **LB. BUTTER**   2 **C. SUGAR**
3 **C. CAKE FLOUR**   4 **EGGS**
1 **TSP. BAKING SODA**   1 **C. MILK**
1 **PINCH SALT**   1 **TSP. VANILLA**
       ¼ **TSP. MACE IF DESIRED**

CREAM BUTTER AND SUGAR, ADD EGGS ONE
AT A TIME, BEATING AFTER EACH ADDITION.
MIX FLOUR WITH BAKING POWDER AND SALT.
ADD ALTERNATELY WITH MILK INTO CREAMED
MIXTURE. ADD VANILLA AND MACE. PUT IN A
GREASED AND FLOURED TUBE PAN. BAKE 1 HR.
AT 350°. WHILE WARM FROM OVEN, BUTTER TOP
AND DUST WITH POWDERED SUGAR.

Grandpa likes it toasted. The "little darlings"
like it any way they can get it. Topped with
ice cream is a favorite.

1. BLACK WALNUT POUND CAKE

TO BASIC POUND CAKE DOUGH ADD
1½ **C. BLACK WALNUTS, CHOPPED**
½ **TSP. CINNAMON**

WHILE STILL WARM, BUTTER TOP AND SPRINKLE
WITH A MIXTURE OF GRANULATED SUGAR AND
CINNAMON.

If possible to hide cake from "darlings," allow to
age a day or two so flavors blend.

76

2. MARBLE POUND CAKE

MEASURE OUT 1¼ C. OF BATTER. MIX WITH ¼ C.
COCOA. PLACE REMAINING WHITE BATTER
IN PREPARED PAN. TOP WITH SPOONSFUL OF
CHOCOLATE BATTER. RUN A KNIFE THROUGH
BATTERS SEVERAL TIMES TO MARBELIZE CAKE.

3. WHITE FRUIT CAKE

TO BASIC POUND CAKE RECIPE ADD:

10	**OZ. DATES CUT AND FLOURED**
1	**C. ENGLISH WALNUTS**
1	**C. PECANS**
1	**C. GOLDEN RAISINS**
8	**OZ. RED CANDIED CHERRIES, HALVED**
8	**OZ. GREEN CANDIED CHERRIES, HALVED**
8	**OZ. PINEAPPLE, CUT IN SMALL PIECES**

LOWER OVEN TEMPERATURE TO 325°, INCREASE.
BAKING TIME TO 1½ HRS IF NECESSARY AFTER.
CHECKING AT 1 HOUR.

COOL. WRAP IN CHEESECLOTH. POUR ½ C. BRANDY
OVER CAKE. PLACE IN A TIN TO AGE A MONTH.
ADD MORE BRANDY TO THE CAKE DURING THE
MONTH TO KEEP IT MOIST IF NECESSARY.

*We gave up putting citron in cake after we caught
one "darling" picking it out of a piece with Chick's
needle-nosed pliers.*

REAL CHEESE CAKE

CRUST

6   OZ. PACKAGE ZWIEBACK
2-3   TBS. BUTTER, MELTED
3   TBS. SUGAR
½   TSP. CINNAMON

CRUMB ZWIEBACK. MIX BUTTER, SUGAR AND
CINNAMON INTO CRUMBS. PRESS MIXTURE INTO
THE BOTTOM AND AN INCH UP THE SIDES OF A
BUTTERED SPRING FORM PAN.

FILLING

1   LB. CREAM CHEESE
½   C. SUGAR
2   TBS. FLOUR
¼   TSP. SALT
1½   TSP. VANILLA
4   EGGS, SEPARATED
1   C. CREAM

MIX THOROUGHLY ALL INGREDIENTS EXCEPT
EGG WHITES. BEAT EGG WHITES UNTIL STIFF.
FOLD INTO CREAMED MIXTURE. POUR ON CRUMB
BASE. BAKE 325° 1 HOUR. COOL CAKE. RUN
KNIFE AROUND EDGE. REMOVE RIM.

*This cake welcomes fresh fruit if a topping is
desired.*

78

COOKIE CUTTER GINGERBREAD COOKIES

5½ C. FLOUR
1   C. SUGAR
1   C. BUTTER
1   C. MOLASSES
3   TSP. GINGER
1   TSP. CINNAMON
1   TSP. NUTMEG
1   TSP. SODA
1   TSP. SALT

CREAM BUTTER AND SUGAR. ADD MOLASSES,
SPICES, SODA AND SALT. MIX IN FLOUR. KNEAD
DOUGH WITH HANDS UNTIL SMOOTH. ROLL OUT
DOUGH ON A WELL-FLOURED SURFACE. FLOUR
CUTTERS. BAKE AT 350° 10 MINUTES.

*Enough dough for a troop of "darlings." Get
out the cookie cutter collection. Lots of fun,
flour and gingerbread people all over the kitchen.
Older "darling" cut out maybe the first gingerbread
Harley. Decorating can wait until another day.
Patience and dough run out about the same time.*

ICING

1   LB. BOX POWDERED SUGAR
2   TBS. BUTTER, MELTED
2   TSP. VANILLA
5-6 TBS. MILK

*Mix to consistency that will be easy for
"darling" decorators to use. Supply colored
sugars, non-pareils, raisins, pieces of dried
fruit. "Darling" will have lots of suggestions.*

CRISP BROWN EDGE WAFERS

½ C. BUTTER
½ C. SUGAR
½ TSP. VANILLA
1 EGG, WELL BEATEN
1 C. ALL PURPOSE FLOUR
  PINCH OF SALT

PRE HEAT OVEN TO 350°.
CREAM BUTTER AND SUGAR, ADD VANILLA, EGG
FLOUR AND SALT.
DROP BY TEASPOON ON COOKIE SHEET. ALLOW
SPACE FOR DOUGH TO SPREAD.
GARNISH WITH A PECAN HALF OR HALF A CANDIED
CHERRY BEFORE BAKING.
BAKE ABOUT 12 MINUTES IN 350° OVEN.
MAKES 3 OR 4 DOZEN DEPENDING ON SIZE

REMOVE FROM COOKIE SHEET IMMEDIATELY

*We put a stop to the performance when we caught
one "darling" dropping dough from the top of a
ladder while another one skated around the
kitchen with a cookie sheet.*

CINNAMON FLOP

GOOD SMELLING PANS COMING OUT OF THE
OVEN MAKE A SPECIAL BREAKFAST. SERVE
FLOP WARM.

2 C. FLOUR
1 C. SUGAR
1 TBS. BUTTER
1 C. MILK
2 C. FLOUR
2 TSP. BAKING POWDER
   PINCH OF SALT

TOPPING

2   TBS. BROWN SUGAR
¼   C. CHOPPED PECANS
1   TSP. CINNAMON
1   TBS. BUTTER

CREAM BUTTER AND SUGAR. MIX FLOUR, BAKING
POWDER AND SALT. ADD WITH MILK TO CREAMED
MIXTURE.
DIVIDE DOUGH BETWEEN 2 CAKE PANS. SPRINKLE
WITH TOPPING. DOT WITH BUTTER.

BAKE 350° 25 MINUTES

JELLY CAKE

1   YELLOW CAKE MIX LAYER
½   C. JELLY OF CHOICE, WARMED

SPLIT LAYER WARM FROM THE OVEN , SPREAD
BOTTOM HALF WITH JELLY. COVER WITH TOP
HALF. DUST TOP WITH POWDERED SUGAR.

*Grandma likes blackberry. "Darlings" love
grape.*

81

1½ C. SUGAR
1 C. BUTTER
3 EGGS
2½ C. FLOUR
1 TSP. BAKING SODA MIXED WITH 1 TBS. HOT WATER
1 LB. CHOPPED DATES
1 LB. RAISINS
1 C. CHOPPED NUTS
1 TSP. CINNAMON
½ TSP. ALLSPICE
1 TSP. VANILLA

CREAM SUGAR AND BUTTER. ADD EGGS, VANILLA, SODA AND SPICES. MIX IN FLOUR. FOLD IN FRUIT AND NUTS. DROP BY ROUNDED TEASPOONS ONTO A COOKIE SHEET. BAKE 350° ABOUT 12 MINUTES.

This recipe takes care of milk and cookie time for many a night unless the "teen darlings" with hollow legs are into the cookie jar. Cookies travel well holding up in lunch bags, purses and brief-cases.

FIZZY JUICE

1   12 OZ. CAN OF FROZEN FRUIT JUICE
1½   QTS. GINGER ALE
1   JAR LONG STEM MARACHINO CHERRIES

MIX JUICE WITH GINGER ALE INSTEAD OF WATER.
ADD A CHERRY TO THE BOTTOM OF EACH GLASS.
WATCH JUICE BEING DRUNK TO GET THE CHERRY.

*We succeeded in weaning them from the baby
bottle. This creation was our effort to wean them
from six packs of soda which we lugged home from
the store. One "darling" grew into teen hood
thinking soda was fruit juice and ginger ale.*

WATER

*A clear liquid known all over the world as a
thirst quencher, except to "darlings." We found
that they will consume some at meals if it is
served in stemware, sometimes with a twist.*

*"Darlings" love stemware, probably
because it's fragile. No explosions at spills.
Accidents happen.*

83

SLUSHY MUSHY

2 **C. GRAPE JUICE**
1 **C. PINEAPPLE JUICE**
1 **C. ORANGE JUICE**
1 **LEMON OR LIME, JUICED**

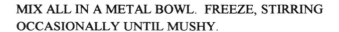

MIX ALL IN A METAL BOWL. FREEZE, STIRRING
OCCASIONALLY UNTIL MUSHY.

*We always figured how and when the "darlings"
served this was their business. In paper cups and
outside was our suggestion.*

COLORFUL PRETZEL DRUM STICKS

10 **THICK PRETZEL STICKS**
 6 **OZ. CHOCOLATE CHIPS, MELTED**
 2 **OZ. NONPAREILS, PUT IN SHALLOW BOWL**

MELT CHOCOLATE CHIPS OVER LOW HEAT. DIP
ONE END OF PRETZEL INTO MELTED CHOCOLATE,
THEN ROLL INTO NONPAREILS.

*Popular with first grade "darlings". Weeks later
we can still find tiny colored balls in hidden places.*

84

BEAUTIFUL WATERMELON JUICE
Truly delicious

PUT CHUNKS OF MELON IN A FOOD PROCESSOR
WITH BLADE ATTACHMENT. NO NEED TO REMOVE
SEEDS. THEY WILL FLOAT AROUND THE BOWL.
PUREE. POUR PUREE AND JUICE THROUGH A
SIEVE, PRESSING WITH A SPOON TO EXTRACT ALL
LIQUID.

*Put juice in a glass pitcher so the beautiful color
can be admired. Do not dilute with anything or the
delicate flavor will be destroyed. The "darlings"
like to freeze the juice in **popsicle molds**.*

FRESH COCONUT

*Work for an adult "darling"---ice pick---sturdy
knife---large hammer---hard surface, preferably
outside.*

*Punch holes with ice pick into dark, smooth areas
at one end of the coconut. Drain milk into container
for all to sample or send to kitchen to use in Thai
recipe. Crack nut with hammer. Pry meat from
shell pieces. Great for "darlings" to experience a
natural treat. Grate left over coconut meat for
another fresh treat.*

AMBROSIA

3-6 ORANGES, PEELED AND SECTIONED
½ TO 1 FRESH PINEAPPLE, CUBED

ALLOW FLAVORS TO BLEND.
SPRINKLE GENEROUSLY WITH FRESH COCONUT.

85

BUTTERSCOTCH

*Eaten over a long period of time it would probably decay teeth, but in celebration of school starting, what the heck. There is something to be said for peace, quiet and a candy binge to repair summer nerves. Just think how nice to have some time to cook without anyone screaming "Mom, she hit me."
Turn on the elevator music, a welcome change from the blaring boom box, and proceed with this* **golden oldie.**

2	C. LIGHT BROWN SUGAR	¼	C. WATER
2	TBS. VINEGAR	½	C. BUTTER
½	TSP. VANILLA		

COMBINE ALL INGREDIENTS. BOIL TO HARD CRACK (310°). REMOVE FROM HEAT; ADD ½ TSP. VANILLA. POUR INTO BUTTERED METAL SHEET CAKE PAN TO HARDEN. **CRACK CANDY WHEN COOL.**

TO GILD THE LILY TOFFEE

1   12 OZ. PKG. SEMI SWEET CHOCOLATE CHIPS
2   C. ENGLISH WALNUTS, CHOPPED FINE

MELT CHIPS; SPRINKLE ½ OF THE CHOPPED NUTS IN A BUTTERED 8"X 8" PAN. POUR BUTTERSCOTCH OVER NUTS. PUT MELTED CHOCOLATE OVER BUTTERSCOTCH. SPRINKLE WITH REMAINING NUTS.

Hide it from everyone!

86

BOW WOW BONES
for the "darling" dogs

2½   C. WHOLE WHEAT FLOUR OR
    2 ½ C. WHITE FLOUR PLUS
     ⅓ C. CORNMEAL
½   TSP. SALT
1   EGG, BEATEN
¼   C. OLIVE OIL
½   C. MILK
½   TSP. GARLIC POWDER
2   OZ. JAR BABY FOOD, BEEF

MIX ALL INGREDIENTS. ROLL DOUGH ¼ TO
½ INCH THICK. CUT WITH BONE SHAPED
CUTTERS. BAKE 350° 25 MINUTES.
KEEP REFRIGERATED.

We baked a tray of tiny pieces to give to the cat.
He only gives us hair balls, but he keeps the dogs
in check. We love him dearly.

A REAL DEAL

Celebrations are an important break in the rut of daily routine. "Darlings" love both fun holidays and solemn occasions.

We increased their number of celebrations by making up a game. We put the name of every country in the world on a small card. Cards are tossed in a large bag. Each "darling" reaches in the bag and pulls out one card. The deal is if they find out which holidays the chosen country celebrates, and why, they can pick one for us to celebrate. Current library cards are an important help.

One little "darling" saved some 4th of July sparklers to help celebrate the Independence day of Bolivia. A lazy one wondered if dog days would qualify. Only the dog agreed.

Holidays can produce great show and tell material. Research pays off. We especially like to celebrate knowledge and understanding.

CELEBRATIONS

BIRTHDAY PIE

The birthday "darling" gets to choose A PIE flavor from the assortment of instant puddings at the store. They also choose the menu for their birthday dinner. However, older siblings may object strongly if the menu is too far out. "Darlings" love special dinners, gifts and especially attention.

CRUST

1   **C. PECANS, CHOPPED**
1   **C. FLOUR**
½   **C. MELTED BUTTER**

MIX AND PRESS INTO PIE PAN. BAKE 350°
15 MINUTES. COOL.

FILLING, *first layer*

1   **8 OZ. CREAM CHEESE**
1   **C. WHIPPED TOPPING**
1   **C. POWDERED SUGAR**

WHIP TOGETHER, PUT INTO COOLED CRUST.

FILLING, *second layer*

2   **PKG. INSTANT PUDDING**
3   **C. MILK**

MIX AND POUR ON FIRST LAYER. TOP WITH
WHIPPED TOPPING.

Candles can be carefully placed around the edge of the pie after it's placed in front of the recipient.

STRAWBERRY CAKE
for GRANDMA'S BIRTHDAY

1 PKG. WHITE CAKE MIX
¾ C. OIL
¼ C. WATER
4 EGGS, DIVIDED
1 PKG. STRAWBERRY GELATIN
1 CUP STRAWBERRIES, DIVIDED

*IGNORE THE INSTRUCTIONS
ON THE CAKE MIX BOX*

TO THE CAKE MIX ADD ¾ C. STRAWBERRIES, WATER, OIL, EGGS AND GELATIN. BEAT THOROUGHLY.

DIVIDE INTO 3 OILED AND FLOURED 8 INCH CAKE PANS. BAKE 350° ABOUT 20 MIN.

STRAWBERRY FROSTING

4 C. POWDERED SUGAR
⅓ C. BUTTER
¼ C. STRAWBERRIES

MIX TO SPREADING CONSISTENCY.

One "darling" wanted this cake with chocolate frosting for his birthday. Skate boarders like to be different. We covered a new skateboard with plastic wrap, put the cake in the middle of the board and had a centerpiece on wheels.

91

EASTER MENU

BAKED HAM
SCALLOPED POTATO CASSEROLE
PLATTER OF SLICED TOMATOES
COLE SLAW
RELISH TRAY
CHUNKY APPLESAUCE
SPOON BREAD
COCONUT CAKE--ICE CREAM

*To enjoy an egg hunt with the "little darling"
consider an--*

EASY EASTER DINNER

HAM	BUY FULLY COOKED, READY TO SERVE
POTATOES	PREPARE THE DAY BEFORE
TOMATOES	A DARLING CAN DO
APPLESAUCE	OPEN JARS, ADD $\frac{1}{2}$ TSP. VANILLA, CHILL
COLESLAW	THE LOCAL DELI'S IS GOOD
RELISH TRAY	ANOTHER DARLING CAN DO
SPOON BREAD	IT'S WORTH DOING, CAN BE DONE AHEAD AND REHEATED
CAKE	THE LOCAL BAKERY CAN DO
ICE CREAM	BUY GRANDPA AN ICE CREAM MACHINE AND THE INGREDIENTS

SPOON BREAD

1¼ C. CORNMEAL
1   C. WATER
½   C. BUTTER, DIVIDED
1   C. MILK
1   C. FLOUR
1   TBS. BAKING POWDER
½   TSP. SALT
3   EGGS, SEPARATED

MIX CORNMEAL AND SALT. BRING TO A BOIL THE
WATER AND ½ OF THE BUTTER. POUR OVER
CORNMEAL. ALLOW TO COOL. BEAT EGG YOLK.
MIX INTO CORNMEAL. ADD FLOUR AND BAKING
POWDER. BEAT EGG WHITES UNTIL STIFF. FOLD
INTO MIXTURE. GENTLY STIR IN THE REMAINING
BUTTER. PLACE IN A BUTTERED 1½ QUART
CASSEROLE. BAKE 30 MINUTES AT 350°.

BANANA SPLIT CAKE FOR A SHOWER

An easy oldie in anticipation of a pretty "new darling":

1   **ANGEL FOOD CAKE** *TUBE PAN SHAPE*, **CUT INTO THREE LAYERS**

       FRUIT

2   **BANANAS, SLICED**
2   **8 OZ. CAN PINEAPPLE TIDBITS, WELL DRAINED**
1   **PINT OF STRAWBERRIES, SLICED**
2   **PINTS WHIPPING CREAM, DIVIDED**
2   **ENVELOPES UNFLAVORED GELATIN**
2   **TSP. VANILLA**
1   **8 OZ. CREAM CHEESE**
1   **C. POWDERED SUGAR**

CONSTRUCTION PLANS

PREPARE FRUIT. WHIP CREAM WITH THE GELATIN AND VANILLA UNTIL STIFF.
MIX 1 C. OF THE WHIPPED CREAM INTO THE CREAM CHEESE AND POWDERED SUGAR FOR FILLING.

BUILDING

PLACE BOTTOM CAKE LAYER ON A SERVING PLATE. COVER WITH 1/3 OF THE FILLING. CIRCLE FILLING WITH ROWS OF SLICED BANANAS, STRAWBERRY SLICES AND PINEAPPLE. COVER FRUIT WITH SOME WHIPPED CREAM. ADD 2ND LAYER OF CAKE. REPEAT PROCESS. ADD TOP LAYER, REPEAT FRUIT. ICE THE WHOLE CAKE WITH WHIPPED CREAM. COVER AND REFRIGERATE OVERNIGHT.

Garnish with chopped walnut and whole strawberries. Serve with chocolate sauce.

94

ST. PATRICK'S DAY-IRISH STEW

A comforting meal to fortify and strengthen for the wearing of the green. "Darlings" love parades.

1½   **LBS. LAMB, BITE SIZE PIECES**
½   **C. FLOUR SEASONED WITH SALT AND PEPPER TO TASTE**
¼   **C. OLIVE OIL**
2   **TBS. BUTTER**
1   **C. RED WINE**
2   **C. BEEF STOCK**
2   **BAY LEAVES**
½   **TSP. THYME**
½   **TSP. ALL SPICE**

COAT LAMB WITH SEASONED FLOUR. BROWN MEAT IN OIL AND BUTTER. WHEN MEAT IS WELL BROWNED, ADD WINE, STOCK, BAY LEAVES, THYME AND ALL SPICE. MIX WELL. SIMMER 30-40 MIN. REMOVE BAY LEAVES.

ADD VEGETABLES

3   **CARROTS, CHUNKED**
2   **STALKS CELERY, 2" PIECES**
2   **TURNIPS, DICED**
4   **MEDIUM POTATOES, QUARTERED**
1   **LARGE ONION, CHOPPED**

COOK UNTIL VEGETABLES ARE JUST TENDER, ABOUT 20 MIN.

Can be garnished with green peas before serving.

INDEPENDENCE DAY
4th. OF JULY CELEBRATION CAKE

1 **C. FRESH BLUEBERRIES**
3 **OZ. CREAM CHEESE**
¼ **TSP. BLUE FOOD COLORING**
1 **14 OZ. CAN SWEETENED CONDENSED MILK**
2 **C. NON DAIRY WHIPPED TOPPING**
1 **TBS. LIME JUICE**
1 **QT. VANILLA ICE CREAM**
1 **PT. STRAWBERRIES**

PUREE BERRIES IN A FOOD PROCESSOR. ADD CREAM CHEESE, MILK, LIME JUICE AND COLORING. MIX. REMOVE FROM MACHINE AND FOLD IN WHIPPED TOPPING. POUR INTO A SPRING FORM PAN AND FREEZE.

TO FINISH ADD A LAYER OF VANILLA ICE CREAM ON TOP OF THE BLUEBERRY LAYER. COVER VANILLA LAYER WITH SLICED STRAWBERRIES. RETURN TO FREEZER. *Garnish with more topping if desired.*

A parade of "darlings" with lighted sparklers strutting around the yard to a Sousa March is quite a sight.

HALLOWEEN HAYSTACKS

12 OZ. BUTTERSCOTCH FLAVORED CHIPS
1½ C. SALTED PEANUTS
1 5 OZ. CAN OF CHOW MEIN NOODLES

PUT THE NOODLES AND PEANUTS IN THE OVEN TO
WARM. MELT CHIPS IN A DOUBLE BOILER. WHEN
MELTED ADD NOODLES AND PEANUTS. DROP
TEASPOONFUL ONTO WAXED PAPER LINED TRAY.
36 TO 48 PIECES, DEPENDING ON SIZE.

*"Darlings" like to prop a pumpkin shaped candy
next to each stack.*

LOLLIPOP GHOSTS

1 BAG OF INDIVIDUALLY WRAPPED
BALL SHAPED POPS--BOX OF
WHITE FACIAL TISSUE
NARROW BLACK RIBBON
MARKING PENS

DO NOT UNWRAP LOLLIPOP

PLACE TISSUE OVER POPS
TIE BOWS WITH RIBBON TO
SECURE TISSUE.
ADD EYES AND MOUTH WITH
MARKING PEN.

97

THANKSGIVING

On Thanksgiving we come together in remembrance
of the Pilgrims, the Indians and their shared feast.
We come together to say our thanks for the pioneers
of all nationalities and cultures who came to this
land each day thereafter. In gratitude we honor all
who have contributed to our country, the melting pot
that nurtures us.

Unlike some holidays there is no agonizing over
what to serve. Turkey is it. The problem is to get the right
size so you aren't eating leftovers forever. We seldom hit
it right. One day applause, the next boos and hisses.
Avoid the temptation of serving turkey leftovers the very
next day. It will lull the "little darlings" into thinking
there are none. Then serve
with pride a rich, elegant favorite, Turkey Tetrazzini.

TURKEY TETRAZZINI

TURKEY LEFTOVERS
8 OZ. SPAGHETTI
1 SMALL ONION, CHOPPED
2 STALKS CELERY, CHOPPED
2 C. MUSHROOMS, SLICED
2 TBS. BUTTER
3 TBS. FLOUR
1 C. MILK OR CREAM
½ C. BROTH OR GRAVY
½ C. ALMONDS, SLICED
1 C. PARMESAN CHEESE
PARSLEY
SALT AND PEPPER TO TASTE

COOK SPAGHETTI AND DRAIN. PUT IN A WELL
BUTTERED 12"x9"x2" BAKING DISH. PLACE TURKEY
PIECES OVER SPAGHETTI. SAUTE ONION AND CELERY
IN BUTTER. ADD FLOUR AND STIR UNTIL ABSORBED.
STIR IN MILK AND BROTH. ADD PARSLEY, SALT AND
PEPPER TO TASTE. ADD MUSHROOMS. POUR OVER
TURKEY. TOP WITH ALMONDS AND PARMESAN
CHEESE.

BAKE AT 350° UNTIL HEATED THROUGH, ABOUT
30 MIN.

PUMPKIN PUDDING

1	29 OZ. CAN PUMPKIN
1	C. LIGHT BROWN SUGAR
1	14 OZ. CAN COCONUT MILK
1	C. GINGER COOKIE CRUMBS
4	EGGS
¼	TSP. EACH CINNAMON, NUTMEG, CLOVE
1½	TSP. GINGER
2	TSP. DRIED ORANGE PEEL

SEPARATE EGGS; BEAT WHITES UNTIL STIFF. MIX
ALL INGREDIENTS, FOLD IN WHITES. BAKE IN A
WELL-BUTTERED 2 QT. CASSEROLE ABOUT 1 HOUR
AT 350°.
GARNISH SERVINGS WITH TOASTED COCONUT,
CHOPPED NUTS AND WHIPPED CREAM.

*Garnishing is a good time job for a "little darling"
because if a little is good, more is better. Although
we thought caramel sauce might be a possibility,
we did veto chocolate sprinkles.*

100

CRANBERRY FRUIT RELISH

1   PKG. RASPBERRY GELATIN
1   8 OZ. CAN CRUSHED PINEAPPLE, DRAINED
1   16 OZ. CAN WHOLE CRANBERRY SAUCE
1   ORANGE, SECTIONED AND CHOPPED
    CHOP ORANGE PEEL FINE IN PROCESSOR
1   APPLE, UNPEELED, CHOPPED

ADD 1 C. HOT WATER TO GELATIN TO DISSOLVE. ADD CRANBERRY SAUCE TO HOT GELATIN. ADD ALL OTHER INGREDIENTS. CHILL OVERNIGHT.

WALDORF SALAD

1½ C. ENGLISH WALNUTS, CHOPPED COARSE
2   C. CELERY, SLICED
3   RED APPLES, UNPEELED, DICED

TOSS FRUIT AND NUTS WITH DRESSING. BEST MADE THE DAY BEFORE SERVING TO ALLOW FLAVORS TO BLEND.

DRESSING

¼   C. MAYONNAISE
1   C. SOUR CREAM
1   TSP. SUGAR
¼   TSP. PAPRIKA

"Darling" sometimes can't remember homework or chores, but any food not repeated from the previous year's feast is missed immediately. New recipes are welcome, but not at the expense of old favorites. "Darlings" love continuity.

101

HANUKKAH

TASTY GOLDEN COINS

½ **LB. SHARP CHEDDAR CHEESE, GRATED**
½ **C. BUTTER**
1½ **C. FLOUR**
2 **TBS. DRIED, MINCED ONIONS**
1 **TSP. WORCESTERSHIRE SAUCE**
1 **TSP. FIVE SPICE POWDER**
1 **TSP. ANNATTO FOOD COLORING**
1 **TBS. SESAME SEEDS**

CREAM BUTTER; ADD CHEESE. MIX IN ALL OTHER INGREDIENTS. ROLL DOUGH INTO TWO LOGS. WRAP AND CHILL. *The freezer hurries the chilling process for "darling" anxious to bake.* CUT COINS 1½" IN DIAMETER, ¼" THICK. *A sturdy size for little hands.*

BAKE AT 350° FOR ABOUT 12 MINUTES ON A LIGHTLY OILED COOKIE SHEET. ABOUT 65 COINS.

If coins are made smaller, adjust the baking time. There could be a sheet of one size made by one "darling" and a sheet of different size by another "darling."

Don't forget to compliment the cooks when this is presented. We all love success, especially "little darlings."

STEAK SALAD *FOR A* WEDDING DINNER

1   **LB. SIRLOIN STEAK, MARINATED, GRILLED, THINLY SLICED**
1   **C. CELERY, SLICED**
½   **C. ONION, SLICED, BLANCHED**
1   **C. MUSHROOMS, SLICED THIN**

MARINADE FOR STEAK

¼   **C. OLIVE OIL**   ½ **TSP. GARLIC POWDER**
1   **TBS. SOY SAUCE**   ½ **TSP. GINGER**
¼   **C. GIN**

MARINATE STEAK 2 HRS. TURNING AFTER FIRST HR. CHARCOAL GRILL STEAK CHILL AND SLICE ACROSS GRAIN.

DRESSING

½   **C. MAYONNAISE**   ½ **C. SOUR CREAM**
¼   **C. PREPARED HORSERADISH**
1   **2 OZ. JAR PIMENTO, DRAINED**
1   **TBS. WORCESTERSHIRE SAUCE**
    SALT AND PEPPER TO TASTE

Toss steak and vegetables. Mound salad on a platter. Pour dressing over salad. Circle with halved cherry tomatoes and baby ears of corn. Sprinkle with capers.

*No one wants to be in the kitchen on Christmas
morning when all the fun is around the tree. Also
tiny "darlings," pets and grandpa might need
protection from possible burial under piles of paper
and ribbon. Set Christmas bread out on a tray and
let everyone help themselves. When all gifts are
unwrapped and disputes start over toys, beat it to
the kitchen to fix the holiday meal.*

CHRISTMAS BREAD

2	ENVELOPES DRY YEAST	½	C. RAISINS
1	C. MILK, WARMED	½	C. CURRANTS
5	C. FLOUR	½	C. SLICED ALMONDS
2	EGGS	¼	C. CANDIED ORANGE
½	TSP. SALT		AND LEMON PEEL
½	C. SUGAR	¾	C. CANDIED RED
½	TSP. ALMOND EXTRACT		CHERRIES
1	C. BUTTER, SOFTENED		

DISSOLVE YEAST IN MILK. ADD EGGS, SALT, ALMOND
EXTRACT, 4 C. FLOUR. BEAT UNTIL SMOOTH. COVER,
LET DOUBLE IN SIZE IN A WARM PLACE, ABOUT 35 MIN.

PUNCH DOUGH DOWN. PUT ON A FLOURED WORK
SURFACE. KNEAD IN BUTTER, SUGAR AND THE REST
OF THE FLOUR. KNEAD IN FRUIT AND NUTS.

DIVIDE DOUGH IN HALF. ROLL EACH ¾" THICK INTO
AN OVAL SHAPE ABOUT 10 IN. LONG, 7 IN. WIDE. FOLD
ONE LONG SIDE OF THE DOUGH TO THE CENTER AND
PRESS IN PLACE. PLACE ON BUTTERED BAKING SHEET.
ALLOW TO DOUBLE. CONTINUED NEXT PAGE

TO FINISH BREAD

BRUSH LOAVES WITH HALF OF THE BUTTER.
BAKE AT 400° 30 MIN. UNTIL BROWN. REMOVE
FROM OVEN, BRUSH WITH REMAINING BUTTER,
SPRINKLE WITH POWDERED SUGAR.

Freezes well--can be made a month ahead.

GOLDEN WALNUTS

2½ C. WALNUTS
1½ C. SUGAR
¼   C. WATER
3   TBS. ORANGE JUICE
¼   TSP. CINNAMON
    GRATED RIND OF ONE LARGE ORANGE

COOK SUGAR, WATER AND ORANGE JUICE TO
240° ON A CANDY THERMOMETER. REMOVE
FROM HEAT. BEAT IN CINNAMON AND ORANGE
PEEL. STIR IN WALNUTS.

*Pour onto wax papered pan. Separate and cool.
Walnuts will be opaque and sugary.*

CHRISTMAS GOOSE
IN A RED WINTER COAT

WASH GOOSE IN SALT WATER, RINSE AND DRY.
USE YOUR FAVORITE STUFFING IF DESIRED.
TIE LEGS AND WINGS SECURELY. RUB SKIN WITH
LEMON JUICE, SALT AND PEPPER. PRICK SKIN ALL
OVER.

PLACE GOOSE BREAST SIDE DOWN ON A RACK IN A
ROASTING PAN. ROAST AT 450° FOR 15 MINUTES.
REDUCE TEMPERATURE TO 350° CONTINUE TO COOK
20 TO 25 MINUTES PER POUND. HALFWAY TROUGH
COOKING TIME TURN GOOSE. REMOVE FAT FROM
PAN. ADD WATER OR STOCK TO PAN IF NECESSARY.
WHEN DONE REMOVE GOOSE FROM OVEN TO GLAZE.
TURN OVEN TO 400°. RETURN TO OVEN FOR 10 MIN.
TO SET GLAZE.

AFTER GOOSE IS PLACED ON A SERVING TRAY, GLAZE
AREAS YOU MIGHT HAVE MISSED, RE WARMING
GLAZE IF NECESSARY.

GARNISH WITH SPICED CRAB APPLES ON PINEAPPLE
RINGS, SUGARED GRAPES AND FRESH PARSLEY.

"Little darlings" have their own name for the dish:
Christmas goose in red winter underwear.
Anything to get attention and giggles from friends.
Whatever they call it, it says Holiday Feast.

RED WINTER COAT GLAZE

1   12 OZ. BOX FROZEN RASPBERRIES
1   TBS. LEMON JUICE
½   C. HONEY

PUREE BERRIES IN A FOOD PROCESSOR. PRESS
PUREE THROUGH A SIEVE INTO A COOKING PAN
TO REMOVE SEEDS. ADD LEMON AND HONEY TO
FRUIT. BRING TO A GENTLE BOIL AND COOK
15 MINUTES. SKIM ANY FOAM OFF AS IT FORMS.
GLAZE WILL BE A BEAUTIFUL DARK RED AND
THICKLY COAT A SPOON.

MERRY   *MERRY*   *MERRY*

MIDNIGHT SUPPER PASTA SALAD

1   12 OZ. PKG. ROTELLE PASTA
4   HARD BOILED EGGS, CHOPPED
2   C. MEAT OR SEAFOOD, CUT BITE SIZE
2   C. VEGETABLES OF CHOICE, SAUTEED
1   C. ROMANO, GRATED IF DESIRED
COMBINE INGREDIENTS, SERVE WARM.

SPICY DRESSING

1   TSP. SEAFOOD SEASONING
1   TSP. CAYENNE PEPPER
1   C. MAYONNAISE
1   TBS. PARSLEY, DRIED
2   TSP. LEMON JUICE
½   C. OLIVE OIL   ¼   C. CIDER VINEGAR
½   TSP. GARLIC SALT   ½   TSP. BASIL

HEAT OIL, ADD SEASONINGS. STIR TO BLEND. ADD
VINEGAR. REMOVE FROM HEAT, COOL SLIGHTLY.
SLOWLY POUR INTO THE MAYONNAISE, BEATING
CONSTANTLY WITH A WIRE WHISK. ADD LEMON JUICE.

BLACK OLIVE CAVIAR

1½   C. BLACK OLIVES, CHOPPED
1½   C. VERY SHARP CHEDDAR CHEESE, GRATED
½   C. ONION, MINCED   ½   TSP. SALT
¼   C. CHILI SAUCE   ¼   C. MAYONNAISE
1   C. PINE NUTS OR PECANS, CHOPPED
1   TBS. WORCESTERSHIRE SAUCE

MIX ALL INGREDIENTS. ALLOW FLAVORS TO BLEND.

NEW YEARS EVE
AT THE SODA BAR

DRESS:
> P.J.'s AND ROBES,
> PARTY HATS,
> NOISE MAKERS.

MENU:
> ICE CREAM SODAS,
> ROOT BEER FLOATS,
> COOKIES.

EQUIPMENT:
> TALL SODA GLASSES,
> ICE CREAM SCOOPS.
> LONG TEASPOONS AND STRAWS.
> CHOCOLATE SYRUP, WHIPPED CREAM,
> ROOT BEER AND SODA WATER,
> MARASCHINO CHERRIES,
> VANILLA, CHOCOLATE , STRAWBERRY
> ICE CREAM.

*When the "little darlings" asked permission to
"stay up" we always said "sure." Few managed to
see midnight. They seem to drop out in order of age.
One was 10 before she saw the ball descending at
Times Square. Never allow confetti without a
designated vacuumer.*

The end

INDEX

Main Courses

Seafood

Fruits and Vegetables

Goodies

Celebrations

ORDER FORM

USE THIS HANDY ORDER FORM TO OBTAIN
ADDITIONAL COPIES OF THIS COOKBOOK.

ORDER AS MANY COPIES OF APRON STRINGS
AS YOU WISH FOR THE REGULAR
PRICE OF $12.95 PER COPY.
MAIL ALL ORDERS TO:
PAWS PRESS
P.O. BOX 331368
ATLANTIC BEACH, FLORIDA 32233-1368

PLEASE MAIL_____COPIES OF APRON STRINGS
PLUS $2.00 POSTAGE AND PACKING PER BOOK
ORDERED. PACKING AND POSTAGE PREPAID
ON ALL ORDERS OF 25 OR MORE COPIES.

MAIL BOOKS TO:

NAME: _____

ADDRESS_____

CITY _____

STATE_____ ZIP CODE_____